MEDITERRANEAN

Air Fryer Cookbook

for Beginners

*2000 Days of Quick and Delicious Recipes to Easily
Cook Meals in Less Than 30 Minutes*

*Includes a Step-by-step Guide to Creating
a Personal Meal Plan*

BY ELLEN RUELL

Table of Contents

Chapter 8
Appetizers and Snacks 75

Chapter 9
Desserts 84

Chapter 10
How to Create a Mediterranean Diet Meal Plan for Optimal Health 95

Chapter 11
Measurement Conversion Chart 99

Introduction

Flavors of the Mediterranean: A Culinary Journey with the Air Fryer

Welcome to a culinary journey where timeless tradition meets modern innovation in the pages of this Mediterranean Air Fryer Diet Cookbook.

The Mediterranean diet, celebrated for its vibrant flavors and numerous health benefits, has been a beacon of healthy living for centuries. It embodies a lifestyle of balance, emphasizing whole foods, fresh fruits and vegetables, lean proteins, and heart-healthy fats, all seasoned with the rich herbs and spices of the region. Now, we bring this age-old wisdom into the 21st century by pairing it with one of today's most exciting cooking technologies: the air fryer.

This cookbook is designed to help you embrace the full potential of combining the Mediterranean diet with the convenience and health benefits of air frying. Whether you're looking to improve your overall health, manage your weight, or simply enjoy delicious meals that are good for you, this collection of recipes offers something for everyone. From succulent seafood dishes and hearty vegetable sides to aromatic herbs and, of course, the essential olive oils, each recipe is crafted to bring the essence of Mediterranean cooking into your home, with the added benefit of modern simplicity and reduced cooking fats.

Our journey will begin with an exploration of the fundamental principles of the Mediterranean diet, understanding why it has been lauded by nutritionists and food lovers alike. Then, we'll dive into the innovative world of air frying, a method that allows us to recreate these traditional dishes in a healthier, quicker, and more energy-efficient way. By marrying the Mediterranean diet with air fryer technology, we aim to provide you with a cookbook that not only guides you through a variety of delicious, easy-to-make recipes but also supports a lifestyle of wellness and vitality.

Prepare to indulge in a collection of recipes that are as nourishing as they are flavorful, all while enjoying the ease and convenience of air fryer cooking.

Whether you're a seasoned Mediterranean diet enthusiast looking for new ways to enjoy your favorite dishes or a curious cook eager to explore healthy eating options, this cookbook is your gateway to a world of delicious possibilities. So, let's turn the page and embark on this deliciously healthful journey together.

So, grab your apron, preheat your Air Fryer, and get ready to savor the vibrant, wholesome flavors of the Mediterranean in a healthier and more convenient way than ever before. Your taste buds and your body will thank you for it. Bon appétit!

Chapter 1

The Mediterranean Diet and Air Fryer Cooking: A Fusion of Tradition and Innovation

In the quest for a healthier lifestyle without sacrificing flavor or convenience, the fusion of the Mediterranean Diet and air fryer cooking emerges as a harmonious solution. This chapter delves into how the rich, nutrient-dense approach of the Mediterranean Diet combines beautifully with the modern efficiency of air frying, offering a path to delicious meals that support well-being and cater to our fast-paced lives.

1.1 What is the Mediterranean Diet?

The Mediterranean Diet is not just a diet but a way of life rooted in the traditional eating patterns of people in the Mediterranean region, particularly Greece, Italy, and Spain. This diet places a strong emphasis on whole foods, fresh vegetables and fruits, nuts, seeds, and healthy fats, particularly olive oil. It includes moderate consumption of lean proteins, primarily fish and poultry, and limited intake of red meat and processed foods. This diet is not just about food but also about enjoying meals with family and friends and leading a physically active life. Key components of the Mediterranean Diet include:

OLIVE OIL
A primary source of fat, rich in monounsaturated fats and antioxidants.

FRUITS AND VEGETABLES
Abundant in vitamins, minerals, and fiber.

WHOLE GRAINS
Providing sustained energy and fiber.

FISH AND SEAFOOD
Rich in omega-3 fatty acids, beneficial for heart health.

NUTS AND SEEDS
Packed with healthy fats, protein, and various nutrients.

DAIRY
Typically in the form of yogurt and cheese, in moderation.

HERBS AND SPICES
Replacing salt with flavor, reducing sodium intake.

RED WINE
Consumed in moderation, mainly with meals.

LEGUMES
Such as chickpeas, lentils, and beans, which are excellent sources of protein, fiber, and essential nutrients.

1.2 Health Benefits of the Mediterranean Diet

The Mediterranean Diet's acclaim stems from its comprehensive health benefits, which include:

REDUCED RISK OF HEART DISEASE
High in healthy fats, antioxidants, and fiber, it supports heart health by reducing blood pressure and "bad" LDL cholesterol levels.

WEIGHT MANAGEMENT
High in nutrients and fiber, it supports satiety and healthy metabolism.

CANCER PREVENTION
Associated with lower rates of certain types of cancer, such as breast and colon cancer.

IMPROVED MENTAL HEALTH
Studies suggest a link between the Mediterranean diet and a lower risk of depression.

IMPROVED COGNITIVE FUNCTION
This may lower the risk of cognitive decline and Alzheimer's disease.

DIABETES CONTROL
Helps control blood sugar levels and reduce the risk of type 2 diabetes.

ENHANCED LONGEVITY
The diet contributes to longer life expectancy by reducing the risk of chronic diseases.

1.3 What is Air Fryer Cooking?

The air fryer, a compact convection oven, has revolutionized home cooking by offering a way to achieve the crispy, fried texture of foods with minimal oil. It circulates hot air around the food, producing a crunchy exterior and tender interior. This technology allows for the preparation of fried foods in a healthier manner, as it reduces the amount of fat and calories without compromising on taste or texture. Air fryers are versatile and can be used to cook a wide range of foods, including vegetables, meats, and even baked goods.

1.4 Health Benefits of Air Fryer Cooking

Air fryer cooking offers several health benefits, including:

REDUCED CALORIC INTAKE

Cooking with an air fryer uses up to 80% less oil than traditional deep-frying, significantly reducing the overall caloric content of the food.

LOWERED RISK OF TOXIC ACRYLAMIDE FORMATION

Frying food in oil can lead to the formation of acrylamide, a toxic substance linked to cancer. Air frying reduces acrylamide formation.

PRESERVATION OF NUTRIENTS

Cooking at high temperatures can degrade many nutrients. The quicker cooking times in an air fryer can help preserve vitamins and minerals.

SAFER COOKING ENVIRONMENT

Without the need for large amounts of hot oil, air frying is a safer alternative to deep-frying, reducing the risk of oil burns.

1.5 The Benefits of Combining a Mediterranean Diet and Air Fryer

Combining the Mediterranean Diet with air frying amplifies the benefits of both, providing a unique blend of health, flavor, and convenience. Here's why this combination works so well:

HEALTHIER FRIED FOODS

With an Air Fryer, you can enjoy the crispy texture of fried foods with minimal oil, aligning perfectly with the Mediterranean Diet's emphasis on healthy fats and whole foods.

ENHANCED NUTRIENT RETENTION

Air frying's quick and precise cooking method means less nutrient degradation, ensuring the fresh ingredients of the Mediterranean Diet retain more of their healthful properties.

ENHANCED FLAVOR WITH LESS FAT

The high heat and fast cooking of the air fryer accentuate the natural flavors of Mediterranean staples like vegetables and fish, reducing the need for excess fats or salts.

VERSATILITY

Air Fryers can roast, grill, and fry, allowing you to prepare a wide variety of Mediterranean dishes while keeping them heart-healthy.

ENCOURAGES PLANT-BASED COOKING

The air fryer excels at cooking vegetables, making it an invaluable tool for anyone looking to increase their intake of plant-based foods.

QUICK AND CONVENIENT

The ease of air frying aligns with the modern need for quick, healthful meals without compromising the dietary principles of the Mediterranean lifestyle. Air fryers can quickly cook a wide range of foods, making it easier to adhere to the Mediterranean diet, even on a busy schedule.

IMPROVED DIETARY ADHERENCE

The convenience and flavorful results of air fryer cooking can help individuals maintain the Mediterranean diet long-term, reaping its health benefits.

The marriage of the Mediterranean Diet and air fryer cooking represents a modern approach to traditional eating principles. It caters to the contemporary desire for meals that are quick and easy to prepare, nutritionally rich, and environmentally sustainable. By embracing this fusion, individuals can enjoy a diverse palette of flavors and textures, support their health goals, and partake in the joy of cooking and eating well. This chapter serves as a guide to integrating these practices into daily life, offering a pathway to a healthier, more flavorful future.

1.6 Mediterranean Diet Shopping List

To help you seamlessly integrate this nutritious and delicious diet into your lifestyle, we've curated a basic Mediterranean Diet shopping list. This list is your guide to selecting the freshest ingredients and pantry staples that will enable you to prepare wholesome, flavorful meals. Whether you're a seasoned home cook or new to the kitchen, this shopping list will ensure you have everything you need to enjoy the full spectrum of Mediterranean cuisine.

So, grab your shopping list, head to your favorite grocery store, and immerse yourself in the vibrant world of Mediterranean cuisine. Enjoy your Mediterranean Diet shopping adventure!

Shopping list

FRUITS:
Apples
Oranges
Pears
Peaches
Berries (strawberries, blueberries)
Grapes
Figs
Dates
Lemons
Melons
Avocado

WHOLE GRAINS:
Whole grain bread
Whole wheat pasta
Brown rice
Quinoa
Bulgur
Farro
Barley
Oats

NUTS AND SEEDS:
Almonds
Walnuts
Hazelnuts
Cashews
Pine nuts
Sunflower seeds
Pumpkin seeds
Sesame seeds
Pistachios
Chia seeds
Flaxseeds

VEGETABLES:
Tomatoes
Kale
Spinach
Swiss chard
Broccoli
Brussels sprouts
Bell peppers
Arugula
Cauliflower
Carrots
Cucumbers
Onions
Garlic
Eggplants
Zucchini

FISH AND SEAFOOD:
Salmon
Tuna
Mackerel
Sardines
Trout
Cod
Sea bass
Tilapia
Shrimp
Mussels
Clams
Calamari
Crab
Octopus
Prawns
Squid

LEGUMES:
Chickpeas
Lentils (green, brown, and red)
Black beans
Kidney beans
White beans
Peas

POULTRY AND MEATS (IN MODERATION):
Chicken (preferably free-range or organic)
Turkey
Beef
Lamb
Lean cuts of pork

DAIRY, DAIRY ALTERNATIVES AND EGGS:
Greek yogurt
Goat cheese
Various kinds of cheeses: Feta, Ricotta, Parmesan, Mozzarella, and many others (in moderation)
Skim milk or plant-based milk alternatives (e.g., almond milk)
Tofu
Eggs

BEVERAGES:
Water
Herbal teas
Coffee
Red and white wine (if consumed in moderation)

OILS AND FATS:
Extra virgin olive oil
Olives (green and black)
Avocado and Avocado oil

HERBS AND SPICES:
Basil
Oregano
Rosemary
Thyme
Cumin
Paprika
Garlic powder
Ground cinnamon
Nutmeg
Pepper

MISCELLANEOUS:
Olives (green and black)
Honey (for sweetening, in moderation)
Dark chocolate (at least 70% cocoa, in moderation)
Vinegar (balsamic, red wine)
Mustard
Capers
Anchovy

This list focuses on the variety and balance essential to the Mediterranean Diet, emphasizing plant-based foods, healthy fats, and moderate amounts of fish and poultry. However, some items can be substituted or added depending on personal preferences, dietary restrictions, and regional availability. Additionally, consulting with a registered dietitian or healthcare professional can provide personalized guidance and help you maximize the benefits of your Mediterranean diet.

Chapter 2

Breakfast Recipes

Note: Nutritional information is an estimate and may vary based on the exact ingredients and portion sizes used.

Mediterranean Omelet Cups

Yield: **6 omelet cups** | Prep Time: **15 minutes** | Cook Time: **12-15 minutes**

INGREDIENTS:

6 large eggs

1/4 cup milk

1/2 cup feta cheese, crumbled

1/2 cup spinach, chopped

1/4 cup sun-dried tomatoes, chopped

1/4 cup Kalamata olives, chopped

1/4 cup red onion, finely chopped

1 teaspoon dried oregano

Salt and pepper to taste

Cooking spray (for muffin tin)

Fresh parsley for garnish (optional)

NUTRITIONAL INFORMATION
(per omelet cup):

Calories: 120 • **Total Fat:** 8g • **Saturated Fat:** 3g • **Cholesterol:** 190mg • **Sodium:** 320mg • **Total Carbohydrates:** 4g • **Dietary Fiber:** 0.5g • **Sugars:** 2g • **Protein:** 9g

DIRECTIONS:

1. In a large bowl, whisk together the eggs and milk until well blended.

2. Stir in the crumbled feta cheese, chopped spinach, sun-dried tomatoes, Kalamata olives, red onion, and dried oregano. Season with salt and pepper to taste.

3. Spray a muffin tin that fits in your air fryer with cooking spray. Evenly distribute the egg mixture among the muffin cups.

4. Preheat the air fryer to 350°F (175°C).

5. Carefully place the muffin tin in the air fryer basket. Cook for 12-15 minutes or until the omelet cups are set and lightly golden on top.

6. Once cooked, remove the muffin tin from the air fryer and let the omelet cups cool for a few minutes before removing them from the tin.

7. Garnish with fresh parsley if desired, and serve warm.

Moroccan-Inspired Breakfast Sausage

Yield: **8 sausages** | Prep Time: **20 minutes (plus chilling time)** | Cook Time: **10-12 minutes**

INGREDIENTS:

500g ground chicken or turkey

1 small onion, finely grated

2 cloves garlic, minced

1 tablespoon paprika

1 teaspoon ground cumin

1 teaspoon ground coriander

1/2 teaspoon ground cinnamon

1/4 teaspoon cayenne pepper (adjust to taste)

1 teaspoon salt

1/2 teaspoon black pepper

2 tablespoons fresh parsley, finely chopped

1 tablespoon olive oil (for mixing)

Cooking spray (for air fryer basket)

NUTRITIONAL INFORMATION
(per sausage):

Calories: 120 • **Total Fat:** 7g • **Saturated Fat:** 1.5g • **Cholesterol:** 60mg • **Sodium:** 320mg • **Total Carbohydrates:** 2g • **Dietary Fiber:** 0.5g • **Sugars:** 1g • **Protein:** 13g

DIRECTIONS:

1. In a large bowl, combine the ground chicken or turkey with the grated onion, minced garlic, paprika, cumin, coriander, cinnamon, cayenne pepper, salt, black pepper, and fresh parsley. Drizzle with olive oil.

2. Mix the ingredients thoroughly until well combined. It's best to use your hands to ensure even mixing.

3. Divide the mixture into 8 equal portions. Roll each portion into a sausage shape, about 4 inches long.

4. Place the sausages on a plate and cover with plastic wrap. Chill in the refrigerator for at least 30 minutes to firm up. This step is crucial for maintaining their shape during cooking.

5. Preheat the air fryer to 370°F (190°C).

6. Spray the air fryer basket with cooking spray to prevent the sausages from sticking. Place the chilled sausages in the basket, ensuring they do not touch each other for even cooking.

7. Cook in the air fryer for 10-12 minutes, turning halfway through, until the sausages are golden brown and cooked through.

8. Remove the sausages from the air fryer and let them rest for a couple of minutes before serving.

Moroccan Spiced Breakfast Potatoes

Yield: *4 servings* | Prep Time: *10 minutes* | Cook Time: *15-20 minutes*

INGREDIENTS:

4 medium-sized potatoes, washed and cut into 1/2-inch cubes

2 tablespoons olive oil

1 teaspoon ground cumin

1 teaspoon paprika

1/2 teaspoon ground cinnamon

1/4 teaspoon cayenne pepper (adjust to taste)

1/2 teaspoon garlic powder

Salt and pepper to taste

1/4 cup fresh cilantro, chopped (for garnish)

1/4 cup sliced almonds, toasted (optional, for garnish)

NUTRITIONAL INFORMATION
(per serving):

Calories: 220 • **Total Fat:** 7g • **Saturated Fat:** 1g • **Cholesterol:** 0mg • **Sodium:** 10mg • **Total Carbohydrates:** 36g • **Dietary Fiber:** 4g • **Sugars:** 2g • **Protein:** 5g

DIRECTIONS:

1. In a large bowl, toss the cubed potatoes with olive oil, cumin, paprika, cinnamon, cayenne pepper, garlic powder, and salt and pepper until evenly coated.

2. Preheat the air fryer to 400°F (200°C).

3. Place the seasoned potatoes in the air fryer basket, spreading them out in an even layer for uniform cooking.

4. Cook in the air fryer for 15-20 minutes, shaking the basket halfway through, until the potatoes are golden brown and crisp on the outside.

5. Once the potatoes are done, transfer them to a serving dish.

6. Garnish with chopped fresh cilantro and toasted sliced almonds if desired.

7. Serve immediately and enjoy your Moroccan spiced breakfast potatoes.

Red Pepper and Feta Stuffed Portobello Mushrooms

Yield: *4 servings* | Prep Time: *15 minutes* | Cook Time: *10 minutes*

INGREDIENTS:

4 large Portobello mushroom caps, stems removed

1 red bell pepper, finely diced

100g feta cheese, crumbled

1 small red onion, finely chopped

2 cloves garlic, minced

2 tablespoons olive oil

1 teaspoon dried oregano

Salt and pepper to taste

2 tablespoons fresh parsley, chopped (for garnish)

Cooking spray (for air fryer basket)

NUTRITIONAL INFORMATION
(per serving):

Calories: 180 • **Total Fat:** 12g • **Saturated Fat:** 4g • **Cholesterol:** 20mg • **Sodium:** 320mg • **Total Carbohydrates:** 10g • **Dietary Fiber:** 2g • **Sugars:** 6g • **Protein:** 8g

DIRECTIONS:

8. Clean the Portobello mushroom caps with a damp cloth and remove the stems. Scoop out the gills carefully with a spoon to create a cavity for the stuffing.

9. In a mixing bowl, combine the diced red bell pepper, crumbled feta cheese, chopped red onion, minced garlic, olive oil, dried oregano, salt, and pepper. Mix well.

10. Stuff each mushroom cap with the red pepper and feta mixture, pressing gently to pack the stuffing.

11. Preheat the air fryer to 360°F (180°C).

12. Spray the air fryer basket with cooking spray to prevent sticking. Place the stuffed mushrooms in the basket, making sure they don't touch each other for even cooking.

13. Cook in the air fryer for about 10 minutes or until the mushrooms are tender and the cheese has melted.

14. Carefully remove the mushrooms from the air fryer and let them cool for a couple of minutes.

15. Garnish with fresh parsley before serving.

Air-fried Greek Spinach and Feta Egg Bites

Yield: *12 egg bites* | Prep Time: *10 minutes* | Cook Time: *8-10 minutes*

INGREDIENTS:

6 large eggs

1/2 cup crumbled feta cheese

1 cup fresh spinach, chopped

1/4 cup red bell pepper, finely diced

1/4 cup onion, finely chopped

2 cloves garlic, minced

1 teaspoon dried oregano

Salt and pepper to taste

Cooking spray (for silicone molds or muffin cups)

Optional: Fresh dill or parsley for garnish

NUTRITIONAL INFORMATION
(per egg bite):

Calories: 70 • **Total Fat:** 4.5g • **Saturated Fat:** 2g • **Cholesterol:** 95mg • **Sodium:** 150mg • **Total Carbohydrates:** 1g • **Dietary Fiber:** 0.2g • **Sugars:** 0.5g • **Protein:** 6g

DIRECTIONS:

1. In a large bowl, whisk together the eggs until well beaten.

2. Add in the crumbled feta cheese, chopped spinach, diced red bell pepper, chopped onion, minced garlic, and dried oregano. Season with salt and pepper to taste. Mix well to combine all the ingredients.

3. Spray silicone egg bite molds or muffin cups with cooking spray. Evenly distribute the egg mixture into the molds or cups.

4. Preheat the air fryer to 300°F (150°C).

5. Place the silicone mold or muffin cups in the air fryer basket. If your air fryer is small, you may need to cook in batches.

6. Cook the egg bites for 8-10 minutes or until they are set and lightly golden on top.

7. Once done, carefully remove the egg bites from the air fryer and let them cool for a few minutes before removing them from the molds.

8. Garnish with fresh dill or parsley if desired, and serve warm.

Air-Fried Zucchini Fritters

Yield:	Prep time:	Cook time:
8 fritters	**15 minutes (including resting time for zucchini)**	**16 minutes (8 minutes per batch)**

INGREDIENTS:

2 medium zucchinis, grated

1 teaspoon salt (for draining zucchini)

2 large eggs, beaten

1/2 cup all-purpose flour

1/4 cup grated Parmesan cheese

1/4 cup green onions, finely chopped

2 cloves garlic, minced

1/2 teaspoon black pepper

1/2 teaspoon baking powder

Cooking spray (for air fryer basket)

Optional: Sour cream or Greek yogurt for serving

NUTRITIONAL INFORMATION
(per fritter, without optional sour cream/ Greek yogurt):

Calories: 70 • **Total Fat:** 2.5g • **Saturated Fat:** 1g • **Cholesterol:** 45mg • **Sodium:** 200mg • **Total Carbohydrates:** 8g • **Dietary Fiber:** 1g • **Sugars:** 2g • **Protein:** 4g

DIRECTIONS:

1. Place the grated zucchini in a colander and sprinkle with 1 teaspoon of salt. Let it sit for 10 minutes to draw out the moisture. Then, squeeze out the excess liquid using a clean dish towel or cheesecloth.

2. In a large bowl, mix together the beaten eggs, all-purpose flour, grated Parmesan cheese, chopped green onions, minced garlic, black pepper, and baking powder. Stir until well combined.

3. Add the drained zucchini to the batter and mix until the zucchini is evenly coated.

4. Preheat the air fryer to 380°F (190°C).

5. Form the zucchini mixture into small patties and place them in the air fryer basket sprayed with cooking spray. Do not overcrowd the basket; cook in batches if necessary.

6. Air fry for 8 minutes, then flip the fritters and continue air frying for another 8 minutes or until they are golden brown and crispy.

7. Remove the fritters from the air fryer and place them on a plate lined with paper towels to absorb any excess oil.

8. Serve the zucchini fritters warm with sour cream or Greek yogurt, if desired.

Greek-Style Air-Fried Pancakes

Yield: **8 pancakes** | Prep Time: **15 minutes** | Cook Time: **16 minutes (2 minutes per pancake)**

INGREDIENTS:

1 cup all-purpose flour

2 tablespoons sugar

1 teaspoon baking powder

1/2 teaspoon baking soda

1/4 teaspoon salt

1 cup Greek yogurt

2 large eggs

1/2 teaspoon vanilla extract

Zest of 1 lemon

1 tablespoon olive oil (plus extra for greasing)

1/4 cup honey (for serving)

1/2 cup chopped walnuts (for topping)

Fresh berries or sliced fruits (for topping)

NUTRITIONAL INFORMATION
(per pancake, without toppings):

Calories: 140 • Total Fat: 5g • Saturated Fat: 1g • Cholesterol: 47mg • Sodium: 160mg • Total Carbohydrates: 18g • Dietary Fiber: 1g • Sugars: 6g (excluding honey topping) • Protein: 5g

DIRECTIONS:

1. In a large bowl, whisk together the flour, sugar, baking powder, baking soda, and salt.

2. In another bowl, combine the Greek yogurt, eggs, vanilla extract, and lemon zest. Whisk until smooth.

3. Pour the wet ingredients into the dry ingredients. Add 1 tablespoon of olive oil. Stir until just combined, ensuring not to overmix.

4. Preheat the air fryer to 360°F (180°C). Grease the air fryer basket lightly with olive oil to prevent sticking.

5. Spoon about 1/4 cup of batter for each pancake into the air fryer basket, forming small rounds. You may need to cook in batches depending on the size of your air fryer.

6. Cook for about 2 minutes, then flip each pancake carefully and cook for another 2 minutes or until golden brown and cooked through.

7. Remove the pancakes from the air fryer and keep them warm. Repeat the process with the remaining batter.

8. Serve the pancakes warm, drizzled with honey, and topped with chopped walnuts and fresh berries or sliced fruits.

Air-Fried Baked Eggs with Herbs

Yield: **4 servings** | Prep Time: **5 minutes** | Cook Time: **8-10 minutes**

INGREDIENTS:

4 large eggs

4 tablespoons heavy cream

1 tablespoon fresh chives, finely chopped

1 tablespoon fresh parsley, finely chopped

Salt and freshly ground black pepper to taste

1/4 cup grated Parmesan cheese

Cooking spray (for ramekins and air fryer basket)

Optional: 4 slices of cooked bacon or ham, chopped (for added flavor)

NUTRITIONAL INFORMATION
(per serving, without optional bacon/ham):

Calories: 145 • Total Fat: 11g • Saturated Fat: 6g • Cholesterol: 195mg • Sodium: 210mg • Total Carbohydrates: 1g • Dietary Fiber: 0g • Sugars: 0g • Protein: 9g

DIRECTIONS:

1. Lightly spray four ramekins with cooking spray.

2. Crack an egg into each ramekin. Pour a tablespoon of heavy cream over each egg.

3. Sprinkle the chopped chives and parsley evenly over the eggs. Add salt and freshly ground black pepper to taste.

4. Top each egg with a tablespoon of grated Parmesan cheese. If using bacon or ham, add it now.

5. Preheat the air fryer to 360°F (180°C).

6. Carefully place the ramekins in the air fryer basket. You may need to cook in batches depending on the size of your air fryer.

7. Cook for 8-10 minutes or until the eggs are set to your desired level of doneness. Keep an eye on them, as air fryer temperatures can vary.

8. Carefully remove the ramekins from the air fryer. Let them cool for a minute before serving.

Air-fried Mediterranean Breakfast Potatoes

Yield: *4 servings* | Prep Time: *10 minutes* | Cook Time: *15-20 minutes*

INGREDIENTS:

4 medium-sized potatoes, washed and cut into small cubes

2 tablespoons olive oil

1 teaspoon garlic powder

1 teaspoon onion powder

1 teaspoon dried oregano

1/2 teaspoon paprika

Salt and pepper to taste

1/4 cup chopped fresh parsley

1/4 cup Kalamata olives, sliced

1/4 cup crumbled feta cheese

1/2 lemon, juiced

Cooking spray (for air fryer basket)

NUTRITIONAL INFORMATION (per serving):

Calories: 220 • **Total Fat:** 10g • **Saturated Fat:** 2g • **Cholesterol:** 8mg • **Sodium:** 200mg • **Total Carbohydrates:** 30g • **Dietary Fiber:** 4g • **Sugars:** 2g • **Protein:** 5g

DIRECTIONS:

1. In a large bowl, toss the cubed potatoes with olive oil, garlic powder, onion powder, dried oregano, paprika, salt, and pepper until evenly coated.

2. Preheat the air fryer to 400°F (200°C).

3. Lightly spray the air fryer basket with cooking spray. Place the seasoned potatoes in the basket, spreading them out in an even layer.

4. Cook in the air fryer for 15-20 minutes, shaking the basket halfway through, until the potatoes are golden brown and crispy.

5. While the potatoes are cooking, prepare the topping by combining chopped parsley, sliced Kalamata olives, and crumbled feta cheese in a small bowl.

6. Once the potatoes are done, transfer them to a serving dish. Squeeze fresh lemon juice over the hot potatoes.

7. Sprinkle the parsley, olive, and feta mixture over the potatoes.

8. Serve immediately and enjoy your flavorful Mediterranean breakfast potatoes.

Sundried Tomato and Olive Quiche

Yield: *6 servings* | Prep Time: *15 minutes* | Cook Time: *20-25 minutes*

INGREDIENTS:

1 ready-made pie crust (9-inch)

4 large eggs

1 cup heavy cream

1/2 cup sundried tomatoes, chopped

1/2 cup Kalamata olives, pitted and sliced

1/2 cup feta cheese, crumbled

1/4 cup Parmesan cheese, grated

1 tablespoon fresh basil, chopped

Salt and pepper to taste

Cooking spray (for air fryer basket and pie tin)

NUTRITIONAL INFORMATION (per serving):

Calories: 390 • **Total Fat:** 29g • **Saturated Fat:** 14g • **Cholesterol:** 180mg • **Sodium:** 500mg • **Total Carbohydrates:** 24g • **Dietary Fiber:** 2g • **Sugars:** 4g • **Protein:** 11g

DIRECTIONS:

1. Roll out the pie crust and gently press it into a greased 7-inch round pie tin that fits in your air fryer.

2. In a mixing bowl, whisk together the eggs and heavy cream until well combined. Season with salt and pepper.

3. Stir in the chopped sundried tomatoes, sliced olives, crumbled feta cheese, and half of the Parmesan cheese.

4. Pour the egg mixture into the pie crust. Sprinkle the top with the remaining Parmesan cheese and chopped basil.

5. Preheat the air fryer to 320°F (160°C).

6. Carefully place the pie tin in the air fryer basket. Cook for 20-25 minutes or until the quiche is set and the crust is golden brown.

7. Once done, carefully remove the quiche from the air fryer and let it cool for a few minutes before serving.

8. Slice into portions and serve.

Greek-Style Air-Fried French Toast Sticks

Yield: *4 servings (16 sticks)* | Prep Time: *10 minutes* | Cook Time: *8-10 minutes*

INGREDIENTS:

4 large slices of bread, preferably a day-old

2 large eggs

1/2 cup milk

1/4 cup Greek yogurt

2 tablespoons honey

1 teaspoon vanilla extract

1 teaspoon cinnamon

1/4 teaspoon nutmeg

Zest of 1 orange

Cooking spray (for air fryer)

Powdered sugar for serving (optional)

Additional honey for serving (optional)

NUTRITIONAL INFORMATION
(per serving, 4 sticks without toppings):

Calories: 220 • **Total Fat:** 5g • **Saturated Fat:** 2g • **Cholesterol:** 95mg • **Sodium:** 260mg • **Total Carbohydrates:** 34g • **Dietary Fiber:** 2g • **Sugars:** 12g (excluding optional toppings) • **Protein:** 8g

DIRECTIONS:

1. Cut each slice of bread into 4 equal sticks, resulting in 16 sticks in total.

2. In a mixing bowl, whisk together the eggs, milk, Greek yogurt, honey, vanilla extract, cinnamon, nutmeg, and orange zest until well combined.

3. Preheat the air fryer to 360°F (180°C).

4. Dip each breadstick into the egg mixture, allowing it to soak for a few seconds on each side. Shake off any excess liquid.

5. Lightly spray the air fryer basket with cooking spray. Place the soaked bread sticks in a single layer in the basket, making sure they do not touch. You may need to work in batches.

6. Air fry for 4-5 minutes, then flip the sticks and continue to air fry for another 4-5 minutes or until golden brown and crispy.

7. Repeat with the remaining breadsticks.

8. Serve the French toast sticks hot, dusted with powdered sugar, and drizzled with additional honey if desired.

Air-fried Halloumi and Tomato Toasts

Yield: *4 servings* | Prep Time: *5 minutes* | Cook Time: *10 minutes*

INGREDIENTS:

4 slices of sourdough bread

200g halloumi cheese, sliced

2 medium tomatoes, sliced

1 tablespoon olive oil

1/2 teaspoon dried oregano

Salt and pepper to taste

Fresh basil leaves for garnish

Optional: Balsamic glaze for drizzling

NUTRITIONAL INFORMATION
(per serving):

Calories: 290 • **Total Fat:** 16g • **Saturated Fat:** 7g • **Cholesterol:** 35mg • **Sodium:** 670mg • **Total Carbohydrates:** 22g • **Dietary Fiber:** 2g • **Sugars:** 3g • **Protein:** 14g

DIRECTIONS:

1. Preheat the air fryer to 360°F (180°C).

2. Brush each slice of sourdough bread lightly with olive oil.

3. Place the bread slices in the air fryer basket in a single layer. You may need to work in batches depending on the size of your air fryer.

4. Air fry the bread for about 3 minutes or until lightly toasted.

5. Remove the toasted bread from the air fryer.

6. In the same basket, place the halloumi slices in a single layer. Air fry for 5-7 minutes, flipping halfway through, until the cheese is golden and slightly crispy.

7. Assemble the toast by placing sliced tomatoes on each piece of bread, followed by the air-fried halloumi.

8. Season with salt, pepper, and a sprinkle of dried oregano.

9. Garnish with fresh basil leaves and, if desired, a drizzle of balsamic glaze.

10. Serve immediately and enjoy your delicious Air-fried Halloumi and Tomato Toast.

Mediterranean Avocado Toast with Za'atar

Yield: *4 servings* | Prep Time: *10 minutes* | Cook Time: *3-5 minutes*

INGREDIENTS:

4 slices of whole grain bread

2 ripe avocados

Juice of 1 lemon

Salt and pepper to taste

1 teaspoon olive oil

1 teaspoon za'atar spice mix

1/2 cup cherry tomatoes, halved

1/4 cup feta cheese, crumbled

2 tablespoons fresh parsley, chopped

Cooking spray (for air fryer)

NUTRITIONAL INFORMATION
(per serving):

Calories: 300 • **Total Fat:** 20g • **Saturated Fat:** 4g • **Cholesterol:** 8mg • **Sodium:** 200mg • **Total Carbohydrates:** 27g • **Dietary Fiber:** 9g • **Sugars:** 3g • **Protein:** 8g

DIRECTIONS:

1. Preheat the air fryer to 360°F (180°C).

2. Spray the air fryer basket with cooking spray and place the slices of whole-grain bread in the basket. You may need to work in batches depending on the size of your air fryer.

3. Cook the bread for about 3-5 minutes or until it is toasted to your liking.

4. While the bread is toasting, mash the avocados in a bowl. Add the lemon juice, salt, and pepper. Mix well.

5. Once the bread is toasted, remove it from the air fryer and let it cool slightly.

6. Spread the mashed avocado mixture evenly over each slice of toasted bread.

7. Drizzle each slice with olive oil and sprinkle the za'atar spice mix over the top.

8. Top each slice with cherry tomatoes, crumbled feta cheese, and chopped parsley.

9. Serve immediately and enjoy your Mediterranean avocado toast with a flavorful za'atar twist.

Mediterranean Veggie Frittata

Yield: *4 servings* | Prep Time: *15 minutes* | Cook Time: *15-18 minutes*

INGREDIENTS:

6 large eggs

1/4 cup milk

1/2 cup feta cheese, crumbled

1 cup fresh spinach, chopped

1/2 cup cherry tomatoes, halved

1/4 cup red onion, finely diced

1/4 cup bell pepper, diced

2 cloves garlic, minced

1/4 cup Kalamata olives, sliced

1 teaspoon dried oregano

Salt and pepper to taste

2 tablespoons olive oil

Cooking spray (for air fryer pan)

NUTRITIONAL INFORMATION
(per serving):

Calories: 250 • **Total Fat:** 18g • **Saturated Fat:** 6g • **Cholesterol:** 280mg • **Sodium:** 450mg • **Total Carbohydrates:** 6g • **Dietary Fiber:** 1g • **Sugars:** 3g • **Protein:** 15g

DIRECTIONS:

1. In a large bowl, whisk together the eggs and milk until well combined. Stir in the crumbled feta cheese.

2. Heat 1 tablespoon of olive oil in a skillet over medium heat. Sauté the red onion, bell pepper, and minced garlic until softened, about 3-4 minutes.

3. Add the chopped spinach and cook until just wilted. Remove from heat and let it cool slightly.

4. Stir the sautéed vegetables, cherry tomatoes, and sliced olives into the egg mixture. Add dried oregano, salt, and pepper. Mix well.

5. Preheat the air fryer to 360°F (180°C).

6. Grease an air fryer-safe pan with cooking spray or the remaining olive oil.

7. Pour the frittata mixture into the prepared pan and place it in the air fryer basket.

8. Cook for 15-18 minutes, or until the frittata is set and lightly golden on top.

9. Carefully remove the frittata from the air fryer and let it cool for a few minutes before serving.

10. Slice into wedges and serve.

Mediterranean Breakfast Burritos

Yield: **4 burritos** | Prep Time: **20 minutes** | Cook Time: **10 minutes**

INGREDIENTS:

4 large flour tortillas

4 large eggs

1/4 cup milk

1/2 cup feta cheese, crumbled

1 cup fresh spinach, chopped

1/2 cup cherry tomatoes, diced

1/4 cup Kalamata olives, chopped

1/4 cup red onion, finely chopped

1 teaspoon dried oregano

Salt and pepper to taste

1 tablespoon olive oil

Cooking spray (for air fryer)

Optional: Tzatziki sauce for serving

NUTRITIONAL INFORMATION
(per burrito, without tzatziki sauce):

Calories: 350 • **Total Fat:** 15g • **Saturated Fat:** 5g • **Cholesterol:** 190mg • **Sodium:** 550mg • **Total Carbohydrates:** 40g • **Dietary Fiber:** 3g • **Sugars:** 4g • **Protein:** 15g

DIRECTIONS:

1. In a bowl, beat the eggs with the milk, salt, and pepper.

2. Heat olive oil in a skillet over medium heat. Pour in the egg mixture and scramble until just set. Remove from heat.

3. Stir in the crumbled feta cheese, chopped spinach, diced cherry tomatoes, chopped Kalamata olives, red onion, and dried oregano into the scrambled eggs.

4. Warm the flour tortillas slightly to make them more pliable.

5. Divide the egg mixture evenly among the tortillas, placing it down the center of each tortilla.

6. Roll up the tortillas tightly, tucking in the sides as you roll.

7. Preheat the air fryer to 380°F (190°C).

8. Spray the air fryer basket with cooking spray. Place the burritos in the basket, seam side down, making sure they don't touch. You may need to work in batches.

9. Cook in the air fryer for 5 minutes, then flip the burritos and continue to cook for another 5 minutes or until they are golden brown and crispy.

10. Serve the Mediterranean Breakfast Burritos warm with tzatziki sauce on the side, if desired.

Air-Fried Lemon Poppyseed Muffins

Yield: **12 muffins** | Prep Time: **15 minutes** | Cook Time: **12-15 minutes per batch**

INGREDIENTS:

2 cups all-purpose flour

3/4 cup sugar

2 tablespoons poppy seeds

1 tablespoon baking powder

1/2 teaspoon salt

Zest of 1 lemon

2 large eggs

1 cup whole milk

1/2 cup vegetable oil

1/4 cup lemon juice

1 teaspoon vanilla extract

For the Glaze (optional):

1/2 cup powdered sugar

1-2 tablespoons lemon juice

NUTRITIONAL INFORMATION
(per muffin, without glaze):

Calories: 210 • **Total Fat:** 10g • **Saturated Fat:** 1.5g • **Cholesterol:** 30mg • **Sodium:** 150mg • **Total Carbohydrates:** 27g • **Dietary Fiber:** 1g • **Sugars:** 13g • **Protein:** 3g

DIRECTIONS:

1. In a large bowl, whisk together the flour, sugar, poppy seeds, baking powder, salt, and lemon zest.

2. In another bowl, beat the eggs and then mix in the milk, vegetable oil, lemon juice, and vanilla extract.

3. Gradually add the wet ingredients to the dry ingredients, stirring until just combined. Be careful not to overmix.

4. Preheat the air fryer to 320°F (160°C).

5. Line the air fryer basket with muffin liners or lightly grease a muffin pan that fits in your air fryer. Fill each muffin cup about 2/3 full with batter.

6. Place the muffin pan in the air fryer basket. Cook for 12-15 minutes, or until a toothpick inserted into the center of a muffin comes out clean.

7. Remove the muffins from the air fryer and allow them to cool for a few minutes.

8. If using the glaze, whisk together the powdered sugar and lemon juice until smooth. Drizzle over the cooled muffins.

9. Serve and enjoy your delicious lemon poppyseed muffins.

Air-Fried Shakshuka with Eggs

Yield: *2 servings* | Prep Time: *10 minutes* | Cook Time: *15-18 minutes*

INGREDIENTS:

1 can (14 oz) diced tomatoes
1 small onion, finely chopped
1 bell pepper, diced
2 cloves garlic, minced
1 teaspoon paprika
1/2 teaspoon ground cumin
1/4 teaspoon chili powder (adjust to taste)
Salt and pepper to taste
4 large eggs
2 tablespoons olive oil
1/4 cup feta cheese, crumbled (optional)
Fresh cilantro or parsley for garnish
Cooking spray (for air fryer pan or basket)

NUTRITIONAL INFORMATION
(per serving):

Calories: 320 • **Total Fat:** 22g • **Saturated Fat:** 5g • **Cholesterol:** 370mg • **Sodium:** 400mg • **Total Carbohydrates:** 15g • **Dietary Fiber:** 3g • **Sugars:** 8g • **Protein:** 16g

DIRECTIONS:

1. Preheat the air fryer to 350°F (175°C).

2. In a bowl, mix together the diced tomatoes, chopped onion, diced bell pepper, minced garlic, paprika, cumin, chili powder, salt, and pepper.

3. Spray an air fryer-safe pan or coat the air fryer basket with cooking spray. Pour the tomato and vegetable mixture into the pan or basket.

4. Drizzle the mixture with olive oil and stir to combine.

5. Cook in the air fryer for 10 minutes, stirring halfway through.

6. After 10 minutes, create four small wells in the tomato mixture with a spoon. Carefully crack an egg into each well.

7. Continue to cook in the air fryer for another 5-8 minutes, or until the eggs are cooked to your desired level of doneness.

8. Carefully remove the pan or basket from the air fryer.

9. Sprinkle the shakshuka with crumbled feta cheese (if using) and garnish with fresh cilantro or parsley.

10. Serve hot, preferably with crusty bread for dipping.

Mediterranean Breakfast Quesadillas

Yield: *4 servings* | Prep Time: *15 minutes* | Cook Time: *8-10 minutes*

INGREDIENTS:

4 large flour tortillas
1 cup fresh spinach, chopped
1/2 cup feta cheese, crumbled
1/2 cup mozzarella cheese, shredded
1/2 cup roasted red peppers, sliced
1/4 cup Kalamata olives, pitted and sliced
1/2 teaspoon dried oregano
2 tablespoons olive oil (for brushing)
Salt and pepper to taste
Optional: 4 eggs, fried or scrambled

NUTRITIONAL INFORMATION
(per serving, without optional eggs):

Calories: 340 • **Total Fat:** 20g • **Saturated Fat:** 7g • **Cholesterol:** 25mg • **Sodium:** 800mg • **Total Carbohydrates:** 30g • **Dietary Fiber:** 2g • **Sugars:** 2g • **Protein:** 12g

DIRECTIONS:

1. Lay out the flour tortillas on a flat surface. On one half of each tortilla, evenly distribute the chopped spinach, crumbled feta cheese, shredded mozzarella cheese, sliced roasted red peppers, and sliced Kalamata olives.

2. Sprinkle dried oregano over the filling and add a pinch of salt and pepper to taste.

3. If adding eggs, place a cooked egg on top of the filling on each tortilla.

4. Fold the tortillas in half over the filling to create a half-moon shape.

5. Preheat the air fryer to 350°F (175°C).

6. Brush each quesadilla lightly with olive oil on both sides.

7. Place the quesadillas in the air fryer basket, working in batches if necessary, and cook for 4-5 minutes on each side or until they are golden brown and crispy.

8. Once cooked, remove the quesadillas from the air fryer and let them sit for a minute before cutting them into wedges.

9. Serve warm.

Greek Yogurt and Honey Parfait with Air-Fried Honey Granola

Yield: *4 servings* | Prep Time: *10 minutes* | Cook Time: *8 minutes (for the granola)*

INGREDIENTS:

For the Air-Fried Honey Granola:

1 cup rolled oats

1/4 cup chopped almonds

1/4 cup chopped walnuts

2 tablespoons honey

1 tablespoon olive oil

1/2 teaspoon cinnamon

Pinch of salt

For the Parfait:

2 cups Greek yogurt

4 tablespoons honey, for drizzling

1 cup fresh berries (strawberries, blueberries, raspberries)

Mint leaves for garnish (optional)

NUTRITIONAL INFORMATION
(per serving):

Calories: 320 • **Total Fat:** 12g • **Saturated Fat:** 2g • **Cholesterol:** 10mg • **Sodium:** 45mg • **Total Carbohydrates:** 42g • **Dietary Fiber:** 4g • **Sugars:** 25g (includes natural sugars from honey and berries) • **Protein:** 15g

DIRECTIONS:

1. In a bowl, mix together the rolled oats, chopped almonds, chopped walnuts, honey, olive oil, cinnamon, and a pinch of salt until well combined.

2. Preheat the air fryer to 350°F (175°C).

3. Spread the granola mixture evenly in the air fryer basket. Air fry for 8 minutes, stirring halfway through, until the granola is golden and crisp. Watch closely to prevent burning.

4. Remove the granola from the air fryer and let it cool completely. It will crisp up further as it cools.

5. To assemble the parfaits, spoon a layer of Greek yogurt into each serving glass or bowl.

6. Add a layer of the air-fried honey granola on top of the yogurt.

7. Add a layer of fresh berries.

8. Repeat the layers until the glasses are filled to the top, finishing with a layer of granola and berries.

9. Drizzle honey over each parfait and garnish with mint leaves if desired.

10. Serve immediately or refrigerate until ready to serve.

Chapter 3

Grains, Legumes and Pasta

Crispy Air-Fried Quinoa Patties

Yield: *10-12 patties* | Prep Time: *20 minutes (plus time to cool quinoa)* | Cook Time: *15 minutes*

INGREDIENTS:

1 cup quinoa, rinsed

2 cups water

2 large eggs, beaten

1/2 cup breadcrumbs

1/2 cup grated Parmesan cheese

1 small onion, finely chopped

2 cloves garlic, minced

1/4 cup fresh parsley, chopped

1/2 teaspoon paprika

Salt and pepper to taste

Olive oil spray (for air fryer)

NUTRITIONAL INFORMATION
(per patty):

Calories: 120 • **Total Fat:** 3g •
Saturated Fat: 1g • **Cholesterol:**
35mg • **Sodium:** 150mg • **Total
Carbohydrates:** 16g • **Dietary Fiber:**
2g • **Sugars:** 1g • **Protein:** 6g

DIRECTIONS:

1. In a medium saucepan, combine the quinoa and water. Bring to a boil, then reduce heat to low, cover, and simmer for 15 minutes, or until the water is absorbed and the quinoa is fluffy. Allow the quinoa to cool completely.

2. In a large bowl, combine the cooled quinoa, beaten eggs, breadcrumbs, Parmesan cheese, chopped onion, minced garlic, chopped parsley, paprika, salt, and pepper. Mix well until the ingredients are evenly distributed.

3. Shape the mixture into patties about 2-3 inches in diameter.

4. Preheat the air fryer to 375°F (190°C).

5. Spray the air fryer basket with olive oil spray. Place the quinoa patties in the basket, making sure they don't touch. You may need to cook in batches.

6. Spray the tops of the patties lightly with olive oil. Cook in the air fryer for 7-8 minutes, then flip the patties and cook for another 7-8 minutes or until they are golden brown and crispy.

7. Serve the quinoa patties warm, with your choice of dipping sauce or as a side dish.

Air-Fried Whole Wheat Pita Chips

Yield: *4 servings* | Prep Time: *10 minutes* | Cook Time: *8 minutes*

INGREDIENTS:

4 whole wheat pita breads

2 tablespoons olive oil

1/2 teaspoon garlic powder

1/2 teaspoon dried oregano

Salt to taste

Optional: Pinch of paprika or cumin for extra flavor

NUTRITIONAL INFORMATION
(per serving, 1 pita bread worth
of chips):

Calories: 180 • **Total Fat:** 7g •
Saturated Fat: 1g • **Cholesterol:**
0mg • **Sodium:** 240mg • **Total
Carbohydrates:** 26g • **Dietary Fiber:**
4g • **Sugars:** 0g • **Protein:** 6g

DIRECTIONS:

1. Preheat the air fryer to 360°F (180°C).

2. Cut each pita bread into 8 equal triangular wedges.

3. In a large bowl, combine the olive oil, garlic powder, dried oregano, and salt. Add the pita wedges and toss gently to coat evenly with the oil and spice mixture. If using, sprinkle with paprika or cumin for additional flavor.

4. Arrange the pita wedges in a single layer in the air fryer basket, making sure they don't overlap. You may need to work in batches depending on the size of your air fryer.

5. Air fry the pita chips for 4 minutes, then flip them and continue air frying for another 4 minutes or until they are golden brown and crispy.

6. Remove the pita chips from the air fryer and let them cool slightly. They will continue to crisp up as they cool.

7. Serve the whole wheat pita chips with your choice of dips, such as hummus, tzatziki, or baba ghanoush.

Air-Fried Stuffed Peppers with Brown Rice and Olives

Yield: *4 servings* | Prep Time: *20 minutes* | Cook Time: *15 minutes*

INGREDIENTS:

4 bell peppers (any color), tops cut off and seeds removed

1 cup cooked brown rice

1/2 cup Kalamata olives, pitted and chopped

1/2 cup feta cheese, crumbled

1/4 cup red onion, finely chopped

1/4 cup fresh parsley, chopped

2 cloves garlic, minced

1 teaspoon dried oregano

Salt and pepper to taste

2 tablespoons olive oil

1/4 cup tomato sauce (optional for topping)

Olive oil spray (for air fryer)

NUTRITIONAL INFORMATION
(per serving, 1 stuffed pepper):

Calories: 200 • **Total Fat:** 10g • **Saturated Fat:** 3g • **Cholesterol:** 15mg • **Sodium:** 400mg • **Total Carbohydrates:** 23g • **Dietary Fiber:** 4g • **Sugars:** 5g • **Protein:** 6g

DIRECTIONS:

1. In a bowl, combine the cooked brown rice, chopped olives, crumbled feta cheese, chopped red onion, chopped parsley, minced garlic, dried oregano, salt, and pepper. Drizzle with olive oil and mix well.

2. Stuff each bell pepper with the rice mixture, packing it tightly.

3. If desired, top each stuffed pepper with a spoonful of tomato sauce.

4. Preheat the air fryer to 360°F (180°C).

5. Spray the air fryer basket with olive oil spray. Place the stuffed peppers in the basket, standing upright. Work in batches if necessary.

6. Cook in the air fryer for 15 minutes or until the peppers are tender and the filling is heated through.

7. Carefully remove the stuffed peppers from the air fryer and serve hot.

Greek-Style Lemon Brown Rice Pilaf

Yield: *4 servings* | Prep Time: *10 minutes* | Cook Time: *25 minutes*

INGREDIENTS:

1 cup brown rice, rinsed

2 cups chicken or vegetable broth

1 small onion, finely chopped

2 cloves garlic, minced

1/4 cup fresh lemon juice

Zest of 1 lemon

1 teaspoon dried oregano

1/2 teaspoon salt

1/4 teaspoon black pepper

2 tablespoons olive oil

1/4 cup fresh parsley, chopped

Optional: 1/4 cup Kalamata olives, sliced

NUTRITIONAL INFORMATION
(per serving):

Calories: 240 • **Total Fat:** 7g • **Saturated Fat:** 1g • **Cholesterol:** 0mg • **Sodium:** 300mg • **Total Carbohydrates:** 39g • **Dietary Fiber:** 3g • **Sugars:** 1g • **Protein:** 5g

DIRECTIONS:

1. In a bowl, mix together the rinsed brown rice, chicken or vegetable broth, chopped onion, minced garlic, lemon juice, lemon zest, dried oregano, salt, pepper, and olive oil.

2. Transfer the rice mixture to an air fryer-safe dish or foil pan that fits in your air fryer.

3. Preheat the air fryer to 350°F (175°C).

4. Cover the dish with aluminum foil or an air fryer-safe lid and place it in the air fryer basket.

5. Cook for 25 minutes or until the rice is tender and the liquid is absorbed. Check and stir the rice halfway through cooking.

6. Once the rice is cooked, fluff it with a fork and stir in the chopped fresh parsley. Add the sliced Kalamata olives if using.

7. Serve the pilaf warm as a side dish.

Mediterranean Farro and Vegetable Medley

Yield: *4 servings* | Prep Time: *15 minutes* | Cook Time: *20 minutes*

INGREDIENTS:

1 cup farro, rinsed

2 1/2 cups vegetable broth or water

1 medium zucchini, diced

1 red bell pepper, diced

1/2 cup cherry tomatoes, halved

1/2 red onion, diced

2 cloves garlic, minced

1/4 cup Kalamata olives, pitted and sliced

2 tablespoons olive oil

1 teaspoon dried oregano

1/2 teaspoon smoked paprika

Salt and pepper to taste

1/4 cup feta cheese, crumbled

2 tablespoons fresh parsley, chopped

Lemon wedges for serving

NUTRITIONAL INFORMATION (per serving):

Calories: 280 • **Total Fat:** 10g • **Saturated Fat:** 2g • **Cholesterol:** 8mg • **Sodium:** 450mg • **Total Carbohydrates:** 40g • **Dietary Fiber:** 8g • **Sugars:** 4g • **Protein:** 8g

DIRECTIONS:

1. Cook the farro according to package instructions using vegetable broth or water. Once cooked, let it cool slightly.

2. In a large bowl, combine the cooked farro, diced zucchini, red bell pepper, cherry tomatoes, red onion, and minced garlic. Toss with olive oil, dried oregano, smoked paprika, salt, and pepper.

3. Preheat the air fryer to 380°F (190°C).

4. Transfer the farro and vegetable mixture to the air fryer basket. Spread it out evenly.

5. Air fry for 15-20 minutes, stirring until the vegetables are tender and slightly caramelized.

6. Remove from the air fryer and transfer to a serving dish.

7. Stir in the sliced Kalamata olives and crumbled feta cheese. Garnish with fresh parsley.

8. Serve warm with lemon wedges on the side.

Greek-Style Air-Fried Barley Risotto

Yield: *4 servings* | Prep Time: *15 minutes* | Cook Time: *30 minutes*

INGREDIENTS:

1 cup pearl barley, rinsed

3 cups vegetable broth

1 small onion, finely chopped

2 cloves garlic, minced

1/2 cup sun-dried tomatoes, chopped

1/2 cup Kalamata olives, pitted and sliced

1/4 cup feta cheese, crumbled

1 tablespoon olive oil

1 teaspoon dried oregano

Zest of 1 lemon

Salt and pepper to taste

Fresh parsley, chopped (for garnish)

Optional: Extra feta cheese for garnish

NUTRITIONAL INFORMATION (per serving):

Calories: 280 • **Total Fat:** 8g • **Saturated Fat:** 2g • **Cholesterol:** 8mg • **Sodium:** 600mg • **Total Carbohydrates:** 44g • **Dietary Fiber:** 9g • **Sugars:** 5g • **Protein:** 9g

DIRECTIONS:

1. In a large bowl, combine the rinsed barley, vegetable broth, chopped onion, minced garlic, chopped sun-dried tomatoes, sliced olives, crumbled feta cheese, olive oil, dried oregano, lemon zest, salt, and pepper. Mix well.

2. Transfer the barley mixture to an air fryer-safe dish or pan that fits in your air fryer.

3. Preheat the air fryer to 350°F (175°C).

4. Cover the dish with foil or a suitable air fryer-safe lid. Place it in the air fryer basket.

5. Cook for 30 minutes or until the barley is tender and most of the liquid is absorbed. Stir the mixture halfway through cooking.

6. Once cooked, remove the barley risotto from the air fryer and let it stand for a few minutes.

7. Garnish with chopped fresh parsley and additional feta cheese, if desired.

8. Serve the Greek-style barley risotto warm.

Mediterranean Chickpea and Vegetable Nuggets

Yield: **20 nuggets** | Prep Time: **20 minutes** | Cook Time: **15 minutes**

INGREDIENTS:

1 can (15 oz) chickpeas, drained and rinsed

1 cup mixed vegetables (e.g., carrots, peas, and corn), finely chopped or grated

1/2 cup breadcrumbs

1/4 cup Parmesan cheese, grated

1 egg, beaten

2 cloves garlic, minced

1 teaspoon dried oregano

1/2 teaspoon paprika

Salt and pepper to taste

Olive oil spray (for air fryer)

Optional: Yogurt or tzatziki sauce for dipping

NUTRITIONAL INFORMATION
(per nugget, without dipping sauce):

Calories: 45 • **Total Fat:** 1g • **Saturated Fat:** 0.2g • **Cholesterol:** 10mg • **Sodium:** 80mg • **Total Carbohydrates:** 6g • **Dietary Fiber:** 1g • **Sugars:** 0.5g • **Protein:** 2g

DIRECTIONS:

1. In a food processor, pulse the chickpeas until they are coarsely ground.

2. Transfer the ground chickpeas to a large bowl. Add the finely chopped mixed vegetables, breadcrumbs, Parmesan cheese, beaten egg, minced garlic, dried oregano, paprika, salt, and pepper. Mix well until the ingredients are combined, and the mixture holds together.

3. Shape the mixture into small nuggets about the size of a tablespoon.

4. Preheat the air fryer to 375°F (190°C).

5. Spray the air fryer basket with olive oil spray. Place the nuggets in the basket in a single layer, making sure they don't touch. Work in batches if necessary.

6. Spray the tops of the nuggets lightly with olive oil. Cook in the air fryer for 8 minutes, then flip the nuggets and continue to cook for another 7 minutes or until they are golden brown and crispy.

7. Serve the chickpea and vegetable nuggets hot, with yogurt or tzatziki sauce for dipping, if desired.

Crispy Chickpea and Herb Falafel

Yield: **15-20 falafel balls** | Prep Time: **15 minutes (plus soaking time for chickpeas)** | Cook Time: **15 minutes**

INGREDIENTS:

1 cup dried chickpeas, soaked overnight (do not use canned chickpeas)

1/2 large onion, roughly chopped

2 cloves garlic, minced

1 cup fresh parsley, roughly chopped

1/2 cup fresh cilantro, roughly chopped

1 teaspoon ground cumin

1 teaspoon ground coriander

1/2 teaspoon chili powder

1/2 teaspoon baking powder

Salt and pepper to taste

2 tablespoons all-purpose flour (or chickpea flour for gluten-free)

Olive oil spray (for air fryer)

NUTRITIONAL INFORMATION
(per falafel ball):

Calories: 60 • **Total Fat:** 1g • **Saturated Fat:** 0g • **Cholesterol:** 0mg • **Sodium:** 80mg • **Total Carbohydrates:** 10g • **Dietary Fiber:** 3g • **Sugars:** 2g • **Protein:** 3g

DIRECTIONS:

1. Drain and rinse the soaked chickpeas thoroughly. Pat them dry.

2. In a food processor, combine the chickpeas, onion, garlic, parsley, cilantro, cumin, coriander, chili powder, and baking powder. Pulse until the mixture is finely ground but not pureed.

3. Transfer the mixture to a bowl. Season with salt and pepper. Stir in the flour until the mixture can be shaped into small balls. If the mixture is too wet, add a little more flour.

4. Form the mixture into small balls about the size of a walnut.

5. Preheat the air fryer to 375°F (190°C).

6. Spray the air fryer basket with olive oil spray. Place the falafel balls in the basket, making sure they are not touching. Work in batches if necessary.

7. Spray the falafel balls lightly with olive oil. Cook in the air fryer for 12-15 minutes, turning halfway through, until they are golden and crispy.

8. Serve the falafel hot with your choice of dipping sauce, like tahini or tzatziki.

Mediterranean Spiced White Bean Croquettes

Yield: *12 croquettes* | Prep Time: *20 minutes* | Cook Time: *15 minutes*

INGREDIENTS:

2 cans (15 oz each) white beans (such as cannellini or Great Northern beans), drained and rinsed

1 small onion, finely chopped

2 cloves garlic, minced

1/4 cup fresh parsley, finely chopped

1/2 teaspoon smoked paprika

1/2 teaspoon ground cumin

1/4 teaspoon dried oregano

Salt and pepper to taste

1 egg, beaten

3/4 cup breadcrumbs, divided

Olive oil spray (for air fryer)

Optional: Lemon wedges and tzatziki sauce for serving

NUTRITIONAL INFORMATION
(per croquette):

Calories: 100 • **Total Fat:** 1.5g • **Saturated Fat:** 0g • **Cholesterol:** 15mg • **Sodium:** 200mg • **Total Carbohydrates:** 17g • **Dietary Fiber:** 3g • **Sugars:** 1g • **Protein:** 5g

DIRECTIONS:

1. In a large bowl, mash the white beans with a fork or potato masher until mostly smooth.

2. Add the chopped onion, minced garlic, chopped parsley, smoked paprika, ground cumin, dried oregano, salt, and pepper to the mashed beans. Mix well to combine.

3. Stir in the beaten egg and half of the breadcrumbs (about 3/8 cup) until the mixture is well combined.

4. Shape the bean mixture into small, round croquettes. Roll each croquette in the remaining breadcrumbs to coat evenly.

5. Preheat the air fryer to 375°F (190°C).

6. Spray the air fryer basket with olive oil spray. Place the croquettes in the basket, making sure they do not touch each other. Work in batches if necessary.

7. Spray the croquettes lightly with olive oil. Air fry for 15 minutes, turning halfway through, until they are golden brown and crispy on the outside.

8. Serve the croquettes hot with lemon wedges and tzatziki sauce if desired.

Air-Fried Greek Gigantes (Giant Beans)

Yield: *4 servings* | Prep Time: *10 minutes (plus overnight soaking)* | Cook Time: *25 minutes*

INGREDIENTS:

1 cup dried gigantes beans (or large lima beans), soaked overnight

1 medium onion, finely chopped

2 cloves garlic, minced

1 can (14 oz) diced tomatoes

2 tablespoons olive oil

1 teaspoon dried oregano

1/2 teaspoon smoked paprika

Salt and pepper to taste

1/4 cup fresh parsley, chopped

1 tablespoon lemon juice

Water for boiling

Optional: Crumbled feta cheese for garnish

NUTRITIONAL INFORMATION
(per serving, without feta cheese):

Calories: 230 • **Total Fat:** 7g • **Saturated Fat:** 1g • **Cholesterol:** 0mg • **Sodium:** 200mg • **Total Carbohydrates:** 33g • **Dietary Fiber:** 8g • **Sugars:** 5g • **Protein:** 10g

DIRECTIONS:

1. Drain and rinse the soaked beans. Place them in a pot with fresh water and bring to a boil. Reduce the heat and simmer for about 60 minutes or until the beans are tender but not mushy. Drain and set aside.

2. In a separate pan, heat 1 tablespoon of olive oil over medium heat. Sauté the onion and garlic until translucent and fragrant.

3. Add the cooked beans to the pan with the onions and garlic. Stir in the diced tomatoes, remaining olive oil, dried oregano, smoked paprika, salt, and pepper.

4. Preheat the air fryer to 360°F (180°C).

5. Transfer the bean mixture to an air fryer-safe dish or foil packet.

6. Cook in the air fryer for 20-25 minutes, stirring halfway through, until the mixture is bubbly and slightly thickened.

7. Remove from the air fryer and stir in the fresh parsley and lemon juice.

8. Serve hot, garnished with crumbled feta cheese if desired.

Spicy Air-Fried Black Bean Patties

Yield: **6 patties** | Prep Time: **15 minutes** | Cook Time: **10 minutes**

INGREDIENTS:

1 can (15 oz) black beans, drained and rinsed

1/2 cup breadcrumbs

1/4 cup red onion, finely chopped

1 small jalapeño, seeded and minced

2 cloves garlic, minced

1 teaspoon ground cumin

1/2 teaspoon smoked paprika

1/4 teaspoon cayenne pepper (adjust to taste)

Salt and pepper to taste

1 egg, beaten

2 tablespoons cilantro, chopped

Olive oil spray (for air fryer)

Optional: Lime wedges for serving

NUTRITIONAL INFORMATION (per patty):

Calories: 130 • Total Fat: 2g • Saturated Fat: 0.5g • Cholesterol: 30mg • Sodium: 300mg • Total Carbohydrates: 20g • Dietary Fiber: 5g • Sugars: 1g • Protein: 7g

DIRECTIONS:

1. In a large bowl, mash the black beans with a fork or potato masher until mostly smooth.

2. Add breadcrumbs, chopped red onion, minced jalapeño, minced garlic, ground cumin, smoked paprika, cayenne pepper, salt, and pepper. Mix well to combine.

3. Stir in the beaten egg and chopped cilantro until the mixture is well combined and holds together. If the mixture is too wet, add a bit more breadcrumbs.

4. Divide the mixture into 6 equal portions and shape each portion into a patty.

5. Preheat the air fryer to 375°F (190°C).

6. Spray the air fryer basket with olive oil spray. Place the patties in the basket, making sure they don't touch. Work in batches if necessary.

7. Spray the tops of the patties lightly with olive oil. Cook in the air fryer for 5 minutes, then flip the patties and continue to cook for another 5 minutes or until they are firm and have a crispy exterior.

8. Serve the black bean patties hot with lime wedges on the side, if desired.

Greek-Style Lemon Garlic Orzo

Yield: **4 servings** | Prep Time: **10 minutes** | Cook Time: **15 minutes**

INGREDIENTS:

1 cup orzo pasta

2 cups chicken or vegetable broth

2 tablespoons olive oil

Zest of 1 lemon

2 cloves garlic, minced

1 teaspoon dried oregano

Salt and pepper to taste

1/4 cup fresh parsley, chopped

2 tablespoons lemon juice

Optional: Crumbled feta cheese for serving

NUTRITIONAL INFORMATION (per serving, without feta cheese):

Calories: 220 • Total Fat: 7g • Saturated Fat: 1g • Cholesterol: 0mg • Sodium: 200mg (varies with broth used) • Total Carbohydrates: 33g • Dietary Fiber: 2g • Sugars: 2g • Protein: 6g

DIRECTIONS:

1. In a mixing bowl, combine the uncooked orzo pasta, chicken or vegetable broth, olive oil, lemon zest, minced garlic, dried oregano, salt, and pepper. Mix well to ensure the orzo is evenly coated with the seasoning.

2. Transfer the orzo mixture to an air fryer-safe dish or pan that can fit in your air fryer.

3. Preheat the air fryer to 350°F (175°C).

4. Carefully place the dish with the orzo mixture into the air fryer basket.

5. Cook for 15 minutes, stirring halfway through the cooking time, until the orzo is tender and has absorbed most of the liquid.

6. Once cooked, carefully remove the dish from the air fryer. Stir in the fresh parsley and lemon juice.

7. Serve the Greek-style lemon garlic orzo warm. Optionally, top with crumbled feta cheese for added flavor.

Air-Fried Mediterranean Vegetable Pasta

Yield: *4 servings* | Prep Time: *15 minutes* | Cook Time: *15 minutes*

INGREDIENTS:

8 oz pasta (such as penne or fusilli), cooked al dente

1 zucchini, sliced into half-moons

1 bell pepper, cut into strips

1/2 cup cherry tomatoes, halved

1/4 cup red onion, sliced

2 cloves garlic, minced

1/4 cup Kalamata olives, pitted and sliced

2 tablespoons olive oil

1 teaspoon dried oregano

1/2 teaspoon dried basil

Salt and pepper to taste

1/4 cup feta cheese, crumbled

Fresh basil leaves, for garnish

Optional:
2 tablespoons pine nuts

NUTRITIONAL INFORMATION (per serving):

Calories: 320 • **Total Fat:** 12g • **Saturated Fat:** 3g • **Cholesterol:** 8mg • **Sodium:** 200mg • **Total Carbohydrates:** 45g • **Dietary Fiber:** 4g • **Sugars:** 5g • **Protein:** 10g

DIRECTIONS:

1. In a large bowl, combine the sliced zucchini, bell pepper, cherry tomatoes, red onion, minced garlic, Kalamata olives, olive oil, dried oregano, dried basil, salt, and pepper. Toss well to coat the vegetables.

2. Preheat the air fryer to 380°F (190°C).

3. Transfer the seasoned vegetables to the air fryer basket. Air fry for 10 minutes, shaking the basket halfway through, until the vegetables are tender and slightly charred.

4. In the meantime, cook the pasta according to package instructions until al dente. Drain and set aside.

5. Once the vegetables are done, mix them with the cooked pasta in a large serving bowl.

6. Sprinkle the crumbled feta cheese over the pasta and vegetables. Garnish with fresh basil leaves and pine nuts if using.

7. Serve the Air-Fried Mediterranean Vegetable Pasta warm.

Air-Fried Pasta Primavera with Mediterranean Vegetables

Yield: *4 servings* | Prep Time: *20 minutes* | Cook Time: *15 minutes*

INGREDIENTS:

8 oz spaghetti or fettuccine, cooked al dente

1 zucchini, sliced into half-moons

1 yellow squash, sliced into half-moons

1 red bell pepper, cut into strips

1/2 cup cherry tomatoes, halved

1/4 cup red onion, thinly sliced

2 cloves garlic, minced

1/4 cup artichoke hearts, drained and chopped

1/4 cup sun-dried tomatoes, chopped

2 tablespoons olive oil

1 teaspoon dried Italian herbs (basil, oregano, thyme)

Salt and pepper to taste

1/4 cup grated Parmesan cheese

2 tablespoons fresh basil, chopped

Optional: Crushed red pepper flakes for extra heat

NUTRITIONAL INFORMATION (per serving):

Calories: 330 • **Total Fat:** 9g • **Saturated Fat:** 2g • **Cholesterol:** 5mg • **Sodium:** 150mg • **Total Carbohydrates:** 52g • **Dietary Fiber:** 4g • **Sugars:** 6g • **Protein:** 12g

DIRECTIONS:

1. In a large bowl, combine the zucchini, yellow squash, red bell pepper, cherry tomatoes, red onion, garlic, artichoke hearts, and sun-dried tomatoes. Drizzle with olive oil, sprinkle with Italian herbs, salt, and pepper. Toss to coat the vegetables evenly.

2. Preheat the air fryer to 380°F (190°C).

3. Transfer the seasoned vegetables to the air fryer basket. Air fry for 10-12 minutes, stirring halfway through, until the vegetables are tender and slightly caramelized.

4. In a large serving bowl, combine the cooked pasta with the air-fried vegetables. Toss gently to mix.

5. Sprinkle with grated Parmesan cheese and fresh basil. Add crushed red pepper flakes if desired for extra heat.

6. Serve the Air-Fried Pasta Primavera warm.

Spicy Air-Fried Pasta Puttanesca

Yield: *4 servings* | Prep Time: *15 minutes* | Cook Time: *15 minutes*

INGREDIENTS:

8 oz spaghetti or linguine, cooked al dente

1 can (14 oz) diced tomatoes

1/2 cup Kalamata olives, pitted and chopped

2 tablespoons capers, drained

4 anchovy fillets, minced (optional)

3 cloves garlic, minced

1/2 teaspoon red pepper flakes (adjust to taste)

1/4 cup extra virgin olive oil

1 teaspoon dried oregano

Salt to taste

Fresh parsley, chopped (for garnish)

Grated Parmesan cheese (for serving)

NUTRITIONAL INFORMATION
(per serving):

Calories: 380 • **Total Fat:** 15g • **Saturated Fat:** 2g • **Cholesterol:** 4mg • **Sodium:** 600mg • **Total Carbohydrates:** 52g • **Dietary Fiber:** 4g • **Sugars:** 5g • **Protein:** 10g

DIRECTIONS:

1. In a large bowl, combine the diced tomatoes (with their juice), chopped olives, capers, minced anchovies (if using), minced garlic, red pepper flakes, olive oil, and dried oregano. Mix well.

2. Preheat the air fryer to 360°F (180°C).

3. Transfer the tomato and olive mixture to an air fryer-safe dish or pan. Air fry for 10 minutes, stirring halfway through, until the sauce is heated through and slightly thickened.

4. While the sauce is cooking, cook the pasta according to package instructions until al dente. Drain and set aside.

5. Once the sauce is done, carefully remove the dish from the air fryer. Toss the cooked pasta with the puttanesca sauce until well combined.

6. Season with salt to taste.

7. Serve the pasta puttanesca hot, garnished with chopped fresh parsley and grated Parmesan cheese.

Mediterranean Brown Rice and Chickpea Cakes

Yield: *8 cakes* | Prep Time: *20 minutes* | Cook Time: *15 minutes*

INGREDIENTS:

1 cup cooked brown rice, cooled

1 can (15 oz) chickpeas, drained and rinsed

1/2 cup breadcrumbs

1/4 cup feta cheese, crumbled

1/4 cup red onion, finely chopped

1/4 cup fresh parsley, chopped

2 cloves garlic, minced

1 teaspoon ground cumin

1/2 teaspoon smoked paprika

Salt and pepper to taste

1 egg, beaten

Olive oil spray (for air fryer)

Optional: Lemon wedges and tzatziki sauce for serving

NUTRITIONAL INFORMATION
(per cake):

Calories: 140 • **Total Fat:** 3g • **Saturated Fat:** 1g • **Cholesterol:** 25mg • **Sodium:** 200mg • **Total Carbohydrates:** 23g • **Dietary Fiber:** 4g • **Sugars:** 2g • **Protein:** 6g

DIRECTIONS:

1. In a large bowl, mash the chickpeas using a fork or potato masher until mostly smooth.

2. Add the cooked brown rice, breadcrumbs, crumbled feta cheese, chopped red onion, chopped parsley, minced garlic, ground cumin, smoked paprika, salt, and pepper. Mix well.

3. Stir in the beaten egg until the mixture is well combined and holds together. If the mixture is too dry, add a bit more beaten egg.

4. Form the mixture into 8 equal-sized patties.

5. Preheat the air fryer to 370°F (185°C).

6. Spray the air fryer basket with olive oil spray. Place the patties in the basket, making sure they don't touch. Work in batches if necessary.

7. Spray the tops of the patties lightly with olive oil. Cook in the air fryer for 15 minutes, flipping halfway through, until they are golden brown and crispy.

8. Serve the brown rice and chickpea cakes hot, with lemon wedges and tzatziki sauce on the side, if desired.

Air-Fried Bulgur Wheat and Spinach Bites

Yield: *18-20 bites* | Prep Time: *20 minutes* | Cook Time: *15 minutes*

INGREDIENTS:

1 cup bulgur wheat

2 cups vegetable broth or water

2 cups fresh spinach, chopped

1 small onion, finely diced

2 cloves garlic, minced

1/2 cup feta cheese, crumbled

1/4 cup fresh parsley, chopped

1 teaspoon dried dill

Salt and pepper to taste

1 egg, beaten

3/4 cup breadcrumbs

Olive oil spray (for air fryer)

NUTRITIONAL INFORMATION
(per bite):

Calories: 70 • **Total Fat:** 2g • **Saturated Fat:** 0.5g • **Cholesterol:** 10mg • **Sodium:** 150mg • **Total Carbohydrates:** 10g • **Dietary Fiber:** 2g • **Sugars:** 1g • **Protein:** 3g

DIRECTIONS:

1. In a medium saucepan, combine bulgur wheat and vegetable broth. Bring to a boil, then reduce heat to low, cover, and simmer for about 15 minutes or until the liquid is absorbed and the bulgur is tender. Let it cool.

2. In a large mixing bowl, combine the cooked bulgur wheat, chopped spinach, diced onion, minced garlic, crumbled feta cheese, chopped parsley, dried dill, salt, and pepper. Mix well.

3. Stir in the beaten egg and breadcrumbs until the mixture holds together.

4. Form the mixture into small balls about the size of a golf ball.

5. Preheat the air fryer to 370°F (185°C).

6. Spray the air fryer basket with olive oil spray. Place the bulgur wheat and spinach bites in the basket, making sure they don't touch. Work in batches if necessary.

7. Spray the tops of the bites lightly with olive oil. Cook in the air fryer for 15 minutes, turning halfway through, until they are golden brown and crispy.

8. Serve the bulgur wheat and spinach bites warm with your choice of dipping sauce.

Air-Fried Red Lentil Fritters (Mercimek Köftesi)

Yield: *15-20 fritters* | Prep Time: *15 minutes (plus additional time for cooling)* | Cook Time: *15 minutes*

INGREDIENTS:

1 cup red lentils

2 cups water

1 cup bulgur wheat (fine or medium grind)

1 medium onion, finely chopped

2 cloves garlic, minced

2 tablespoons tomato paste

2 tablespoons olive oil

1 teaspoon paprika

1/2 teaspoon ground cumin

1/4 teaspoon cayenne pepper (adjust to taste)

Salt and pepper to taste

1/4 cup fresh parsley, finely chopped

1/4 cup green onions, finely chopped

Olive oil spray (for air fryer)

Lemon wedges for serving

DIRECTIONS:

1. Rinse the red lentils and place them in a pot with 2 cups of water. Bring to a boil, then reduce the heat and simmer until the lentils are soft and the water is absorbed about 15-20 minutes.

2. Remove the pot from the heat and stir in the bulgur wheat. Cover and let it sit for about 15 minutes, allowing the bulgur to absorb the remaining moisture and soften.

3. In a skillet, heat 2 tablespoons of olive oil over medium heat. Sauté the onion and garlic until translucent. Add the tomato paste, paprika, cumin, cayenne pepper, salt, and pepper. Cook for another 2 minutes.

4. Combine the lentil and bulgur mixture with the onion mixture in a large bowl. Mix well. Allow the mixture to cool to room temperature.

5. Once cooled, stir in the chopped parsley and green onions. Mix until well combined.

6. Preheat the air fryer to 360°F (180°C).

7. Shape the mixture into small, oval fritters.

NUTRITIONAL INFORMATION
(per fritter):

Calories: 70 • **Total Fat:** 1.5g •
Saturated Fat: 0.2g • **Cholesterol:**
0mg • **Sodium:** 10mg • **Total**
Carbohydrates: 12g • **Dietary Fiber:**
3g • **Sugars:** 0.5g • **Protein:** 3g

8. Spray the air fryer basket with olive oil spray. Place the fritters in the basket, making sure they don't touch each other. Work in batches if necessary.

9. Spray the fritters lightly with olive oil. Cook in the air fryer for 15 minutes, turning halfway through, until they are golden and slightly crispy.

10. Serve the red lentil fritters hot with lemon wedges on the side.

Air-Fried Lentil Koftas

Yield: *12-15 koftas* | Prep Time: *20 minutes (plus time for lentils to cool)* | Cook Time: *15 minutes*

INGREDIENTS:

1 cup dried red lentils

2 cups water

1 small onion, finely chopped

2 cloves garlic, minced

1 carrot, grated

1/4 cup fresh parsley, chopped

1 teaspoon ground cumin

1/2 teaspoon ground coriander

1/2 teaspoon paprika

1/4 teaspoon cayenne pepper
(adjust to taste)

Salt and pepper to taste

1/2 cup breadcrumbs

1 egg, beaten

Olive oil spray (for air fryer)

NUTRITIONAL INFORMATION
(per kofta):

Calories: 80 • **Total Fat:** 1g •
Saturated Fat: 0g • **Cholesterol:**
15mg • **Sodium:** 50mg • **Total**
Carbohydrates: 12g • **Dietary Fiber:**
3g • **Sugars:** 1g • **Protein:** 5g

DIRECTIONS:

1. Rinse the lentils and place them in a saucepan with 2 cups of water. Bring to a boil, then reduce heat and simmer for about 15 minutes or until lentils are soft and the water is absorbed. Let the lentils cool.

2. In a large bowl, mash the cooled lentils with a fork or potato masher.

3. Add the chopped onion, minced garlic, grated carrot, chopped parsley, cumin, coriander, paprika, cayenne pepper, salt, and pepper to the mashed lentils. Mix well.

4. Stir in the breadcrumbs and beaten egg until the mixture is well combined and can be shaped into small oval koftas.

5. Preheat the air fryer to 375°F (190°C).

6. Shape the lentil mixture into small oval koftas, about 2 inches long.

7. Spray the air fryer basket with olive oil spray. Place the koftas in the basket, making sure they are not touching. Work in batches if necessary.

8. Spray the koftas lightly with olive oil. Cook in the air fryer for 15 minutes, turning halfway through, until they are golden and crispy.

9. Serve the lentil koftas hot with your choice of dipping sauce or as part of a Mediterranean-inspired meal.

Chapter 4

Vegetables

Roasted Air-Fried Carrots with Honey and Thyme

Yield: *4 servings* | Prep Time: *10 minutes* | Cook Time: *15 minutes*

INGREDIENTS:

1 pound carrots, peeled and sliced into 1/4-inch thick sticks

2 tablespoons olive oil

2 tablespoons honey

1 tablespoon fresh thyme leaves, chopped (or 1 teaspoon dried thyme)

Salt and pepper to taste

NUTRITIONAL INFORMATION (per serving):

Calories: 140 • **Total Fat:** 7g • **Saturated Fat:** 1g • **Cholesterol:** 0mg • **Sodium:** 85mg • **Total Carbohydrates:** 20g • **Dietary Fiber:** 3g • **Sugars:** 14g (includes 9g added sugars from honey) • **Protein:** 1g

DIRECTIONS:

1. **Prepare the Carrots:** In a large bowl, toss the sliced carrots with olive oil, honey, thyme, salt, and pepper until well coated.

2. Preheat the air fryer to 380°F (190°C).

3. **Air Fry the Carrots:**

   a. Arrange the carrots in the air fryer basket in a single layer. You may need to cook in batches to avoid overcrowding.

   b. Air fry for 15 minutes, shaking the basket halfway through until the carrots are tender and caramelized.

4. **Serve:** Transfer the roasted carrots to a serving dish. If desired, drizzle with a little more honey and sprinkle with additional fresh thyme before serving.

Mediterranean Air-Fried Eggplant Bites

Yield: *4 servings* | Prep Time: *15 minutes* | Cook Time: *10 minutes*

INGREDIENTS:

1 medium eggplant, cut into 1/2-inch cubes

1/2 cup all-purpose flour

2 large eggs, beaten

1 cup breadcrumbs

1/2 cup grated Parmesan cheese

1 teaspoon dried oregano

1/2 teaspoon garlic powder

Salt and pepper to taste

Olive oil spray (for air frying)

Marinara sauce, for serving

NUTRITIONAL INFORMATION (per serving):

Calories: 280 • **Total Fat:** 8g • **Saturated Fat:** 3g • **Cholesterol:** 95mg • **Sodium:** 400mg • **Total Carbohydrates:** 38g • **Dietary Fiber:** 5g • **Sugars:** 6g • **Protein:** 14g

DIRECTIONS:

1. **Prep the Eggplant:** Place the eggplant cubes in a colander and sprinkle with salt. Let sit for 10 minutes to draw out moisture. Rinse with water and pat dry with paper towels.

2. **Breading Station: Set up three shallow bowls:** one with the flour, one with the beaten eggs, and one with a mixture of breadcrumbs, grated Parmesan cheese, dried oregano, garlic powder, salt, and pepper.

3. **Coat the Eggplant:** Dredge the eggplant cubes first in flour, shaking off the excess, then dip in the beaten eggs, and finally coat in the breadcrumb mixture.

4. Preheat the air fryer to 390°F (200°C).

5. **Air Fry the Eggplant:**

   a. Spray the air fryer basket with olive oil spray. Arrange the breaded eggplant cubes in the basket in a single layer, making sure they do not touch. You may need to cook in batches.

   b. Spray the tops of the eggplant cubes lightly with olive oil. Air fry for 10 minutes or until golden brown and crispy, shaking the basket halfway through cooking.

6. Serve the air-fried eggplant Parmesan bites hot with marinara sauce on the side for dipping.

Lemon Garlic Air-Fried Asparagus

Yield: **4 servings** | Prep Time: **5 minutes** | Cook Time: **8 minutes**

INGREDIENTS:

1 pound fresh asparagus, ends trimmed

2 tablespoons olive oil

2 cloves garlic, minced

Zest of 1 lemon

2 tablespoons lemon juice

Salt and pepper to taste

Optional: Grated Parmesan cheese for garnish

NUTRITIONAL INFORMATION
(per serving):

Calories: 90 • **Total Fat:** 7g • **Saturated Fat:** 1g • **Cholesterol:** 0mg • **Sodium:** 150mg • **Total Carbohydrates:** 6g • **Dietary Fiber:** 3g • **Sugars:** 3g • **Protein:** 3g

DIRECTIONS:

1. **Season the Asparagus:** In a large bowl, toss the asparagus spears with olive oil, minced garlic, lemon zest, lemon juice, salt, and pepper until they are evenly coated.

2. Preheat the air fryer to 400°F (200°C).

3. **Air Fry the Asparagus:**

   a. Arrange the asparagus in the air fryer basket in a single layer. Depending on the size of your air fryer, you may need to cook the asparagus in batches.

   b. Air fry for 7-8 minutes or until the asparagus is tender and lightly browned at the tips.

4. **Serve:** Transfer the air-fried asparagus to a serving plate. If desired, sprinkle with grated Parmesan cheese while the asparagus is still hot. Serve immediately as a flavorful and healthy side dish.

Air-Fried Ratatouille (Mixed Mediterranean Vegetables)

Yield: **4 servings** | Prep Time: **20 minutes** | Cook Time: **15 minutes**

INGREDIENTS:

1 small eggplant, cut into 1/2-inch cubes

1 medium zucchini, cut into 1/2-inch cubes

1 medium yellow squash, cut into 1/2-inch cubes

1 red bell pepper, cut into 1/2-inch pieces

1 yellow bell pepper, cut into 1/2-inch pieces

1 small red onion, cut into wedges

3 tablespoons olive oil

2 cloves garlic, minced

1 teaspoon dried thyme

1/2 teaspoon dried oregano

Salt and pepper to taste

1 cup cherry tomatoes, halved

Fresh basil leaves for garnish

NUTRITIONAL INFORMATION
(per serving):

Calories: 150 • **Total Fat:** 10g • **Saturated Fat:** 1.5g • **Cholesterol:** 0mg • **Sodium:** 75mg • **Total Carbohydrates:** 14g • **Dietary Fiber:** 5g • **Sugars:** 8g • **Protein:** 3g

DIRECTIONS:

1. **Prep the Vegetables:** In a large bowl, combine eggplant, zucchini, yellow squash, red bell pepper, yellow bell pepper, and red onion.

2. **Season the Vegetables:** Add olive oil, minced garlic, thyme, oregano, salt, and pepper to the bowl with the vegetables. Toss until all the vegetables are evenly coated with the oil and seasonings.

3. Preheat the air fryer to 400°F (200°C).

4. **Air Fry the Vegetables:**

   a. Transfer the seasoned vegetables (excluding cherry tomatoes) to the air fryer basket, spreading them out into a single layer. Depending on the size of your air fryer, you may need to cook in batches.

   b. Air fry for 10 minutes, shaking the basket halfway through.

5. **Add Cherry Tomatoes:** After 10 minutes, add the cherry tomatoes to the basket and toss with the other vegetables. Continue to air fry for an additional 5 minutes or until all the vegetables are tender and slightly browned.

6. **Serve:** Transfer the air-fried ratatouille to a serving dish. Garnish with fresh basil leaves before serving.

Spiced Air-Fried Eggplant Slices with Yogurt Sauce

Yield: *4 servings* | Prep Time: *15 minutes (includes salting time)* | Cook Time: *12 minutes*

INGREDIENTS:

For Eggplant Slices:
2 medium eggplants, sliced into 1/2-inch rounds
Salt, for drawing out moisture
2 tablespoons olive oil
1 teaspoon ground cumin
1/2 teaspoon smoked paprika
1/4 teaspoon ground coriander
1/4 teaspoon garlic powder
Black pepper to taste

For Yogurt Sauce:
1 cup plain Greek yogurt
2 tablespoons fresh lemon juice
1 clove garlic, minced
1 tablespoon fresh mint, finely chopped
Salt and pepper to taste

NUTRITIONAL INFORMATION (per serving):
Calories: 180 • Total Fat: 8g • Saturated Fat: 1g • Cholesterol: 5mg • Sodium: 80mg (varies depending on how much salt is washed off) • Total Carbohydrates: 22g • Dietary Fiber: 9g • Sugars: 12g • Protein: 8g

DIRECTIONS:

1. **Salt the Eggplant:** Lay the eggplant slices in a single layer on paper towels and sprinkle both sides with salt. Let them sit for 10 minutes to draw out moisture, then pat dry with additional paper towels.

2. **Season the Eggplant:** In a small bowl, mix together cumin, smoked paprika, coriander, garlic powder, and black pepper. Brush both sides of the eggplant slices with olive oil, then evenly sprinkle the spice mixture on each side.

3. Preheat the air fryer to 380°F (190°C).

4. **Air Fry the Eggplant:** Arrange the eggplant slices in the air fryer basket in a single layer, working in batches if necessary. Air fry for 6 minutes on each side, or until the eggplant is tender and the edges are slightly crispy.

5. **Prepare the Yogurt Sauce:** While the eggplant is cooking, prepare the yogurt sauce by combining Greek yogurt, lemon juice, minced garlic, chopped mint, salt, and pepper in a bowl. Stir until smooth and well combined.

6. Serve the air-fried eggplant slices immediately with the yogurt sauce on the side for dipping.

Air-Fried Sweet Potato Wedges with Tzatziki

Yield: *4 servings* | Prep Time: *10 minutes* | Cook Time: *20 minutes*

INGREDIENTS:

For Sweet Potato Wedges:
2 large sweet potatoes, washed and cut into wedges
2 tablespoons olive oil
1 teaspoon smoked paprika
1/2 teaspoon garlic powder
Salt and pepper to taste

For Tzatziki:
1 cup Greek yogurt
1/2 cucumber, finely grated and squeezed to remove excess water
2 cloves garlic, minced
1 tablespoon lemon juice
1 tablespoon fresh dill, chopped (or 1 teaspoon dried dill)
Salt and pepper to taste

NUTRITIONAL INFORMATION (per serving):
Calories: 220 • Total Fat: 8g • Saturated Fat: 1g • Cholesterol: 5mg • Sodium: 120mg • Total Carbohydrates: 31g • Dietary Fiber: 5g • Sugars: 9g • Protein: 7g

DIRECTIONS:

1. **Prep the Sweet Potatoes:** Toss the sweet potato wedges with olive oil, smoked paprika, garlic powder, salt, and pepper until well coated.

2. Preheat the air fryer to 400°F (200°C).

3. **Air Fry the Sweet Potatoes:**
   a. Arrange the sweet potato wedges in the air fryer basket in a single layer. You may need to cook in batches depending on the size of your air fryer.
   b. Air fry for 20 minutes, turning halfway through, until the wedges are crispy on the outside and tender on the inside.

4. **Prepare the Tzatziki:** While the sweet potatoes are cooking, prepare the tzatziki sauce. In a bowl, combine Greek yogurt, grated cucumber, minced garlic, lemon juice, dill, salt, and pepper. Mix well until smooth. Adjust seasoning as needed.

5. Serve the air-fried sweet potato wedges hot with the tzatziki sauce on the side for dipping.

Air-Fried Butternut Squash with Sage

Yield: *4 servings* | Prep Time: *15 minutes* | Cook Time: *20 minutes*

INGREDIENTS:

1 medium butternut squash (about 2 pounds), peeled, seeded, and cut into 1-inch cubes

2 tablespoons olive oil

1 tablespoon fresh sage, finely chopped

Salt and pepper to taste

Optional: Pinch of nutmeg

Optional: Grated Parmesan cheese for serving

NUTRITIONAL INFORMATION (per serving):

Calories: 140 • **Total Fat:** 7g • **Saturated Fat:** 1g • **Cholesterol:** 0mg • **Sodium:** 10mg • **Total Carbohydrates:** 20g • **Dietary Fiber:** 3g • **Sugars:** 4g • **Protein:** 2g

DIRECTIONS:

1. **Prep the Butternut Squash:** Start by peeling the butternut squash, removing the seeds, and cutting it into 1-inch cubes. Try to keep the pieces uniform for even cooking.

2. **Season the Squash:** In a large bowl, toss the butternut squash cubes with olive oil, chopped sage, salt, pepper, and a pinch of nutmeg, if using, until well coated.

3. Preheat the air fryer to 380°F (190°C).

4. **Air Fry the Squash:**

   a. Arrange the seasoned butternut squash in the air fryer basket in a single layer. Depending on the size of your air fryer, you may need to cook in batches.

   b. Air fry for 20 minutes, shaking the basket halfway through, until the squash is tender and the edges are starting to caramelize.

5. **Serve:** Transfer the air-fried butternut squash to a serving dish. Optionally, sprinkle with grated Parmesan cheese while still hot. Serve immediately as a flavorful and healthy side dish.

Air-Fried Green Beans with Almond Slivers

Yield: *4 servings* | Prep Time: *10 minutes* | Cook Time: *10 minutes*

INGREDIENTS:

1 pound fresh green beans, ends trimmed

1 tablespoon olive oil

Salt and pepper to taste

1/4 cup almond slivers

1 teaspoon lemon zest

1 tablespoon lemon juice

Optional: Garlic powder to taste

NUTRITIONAL INFORMATION (per serving):

Calories: 100 • **Total Fat:** 7g • **Saturated Fat:** 1g • **Cholesterol:** 0mg • **Sodium:** 10mg • **Total Carbohydrates:** 9g • **Dietary Fiber:** 4g • **Sugars:** 3g • **Protein:** 3g

DIRECTIONS:

1. **Prep the Green Beans:** Rinse the green beans and trim the ends. Pat dry to remove excess moisture.

2. **Season the Green Beans:** In a large bowl, toss the green beans with olive oil, salt, pepper, and optional garlic powder until well coated.

3. Preheat the air fryer to 380°F (190°C).

4. **Air Fry the Green Beans:** Transfer the seasoned green beans to the air fryer basket. Air fry for 7 minutes, shaking the basket halfway through the cooking time.

5. **Add Almonds:** After 7 minutes, sprinkle the almond slivers over the green beans. Continue to air fry for an additional 3 minutes or until the green beans are tender and the almonds are lightly toasted.

6. **Finish with Lemon:** Once done, transfer the green beans and almonds to a serving dish. Drizzle with lemon juice and sprinkle with lemon zest.

7. Serve immediately as a delicious and nutritious side dish.

Air-Fried Asparagus with Lemon and Feta

Yield: *4 servings* | Prep Time: *5 minutes* | Cook Time: *8 minutes*

INGREDIENTS:

1 pound fresh asparagus, ends trimmed

2 tablespoons olive oil

Salt and pepper to taste

Zest of 1 lemon

2 tablespoons lemon juice

1/4 cup feta cheese, crumbled

Optional: Fresh dill or parsley for garnish

NUTRITIONAL INFORMATION
(per serving):

Calories: 110 • **Total Fat:** 8g • **Saturated Fat:** 2g • **Cholesterol:** 8mg • **Sodium:** 125mg • **Total Carbohydrates:** 6g • **Dietary Fiber:** 2g • **Sugars:** 3g • **Protein:** 4g

DIRECTIONS:

1. **Prep the Asparagus:** Rinse the asparagus and trim off the tough ends. Pat dry with paper towels.

2. **Season the Asparagus:** In a large bowl, toss the asparagus with olive oil, salt, and pepper until evenly coated.

3. Preheat the air fryer to 400°F (200°C).

4. **Air Fry the Asparagus:**

   a. Arrange the asparagus in the air fryer basket in a single layer. Depending on the size of your air fryer, you may need to cook in batches.

   b. Air fry for 7-8 minutes or until the asparagus is tender and slightly crispy at the tips.

5. **Add Lemon and Feta:** Once cooked, transfer the asparagus to a serving plate. Sprinkle with lemon zest and drizzle with lemon juice. Top with crumbled feta cheese.

6. **Serve:** If desired, garnish with fresh dill or parsley before serving. Serve immediately.

Garlic and Herb Air-Fried Mushrooms

Yield: *4 servings* | Prep Time: *10 minutes* | Cook Time: *12 minutes*

INGREDIENTS:

1 pound button mushrooms, cleaned and stems trimmed

3 tablespoons olive oil

4 cloves garlic, minced

1 tablespoon fresh thyme, chopped (or 1 teaspoon dried thyme)

1 tablespoon fresh rosemary, chopped (or 1 teaspoon dried rosemary)

Salt and pepper to taste

Optional: Fresh parsley, chopped for garnish

NUTRITIONAL INFORMATION
((per serving):

Calories: 120 • **Total Fat:** 10g • **Saturated Fat:** 1.5g • **Cholesterol:** 0mg • **Sodium:** 10mg • **Total Carbohydrates:** 6g • **Dietary Fiber:** 2g • **Sugars:** 2g • **Protein:** 3g

DIRECTIONS:

1. **Prep the Mushrooms:** In a large bowl, combine the mushrooms, olive oil, minced garlic, thyme, rosemary, salt, and pepper. Toss until the mushrooms are evenly coated with the oil and herbs.

2. Preheat the air fryer to 380°F (190°C).

3. **Air Fry the Mushrooms:**

   a. Transfer the seasoned mushrooms to the air fryer basket. Spread them out into a single layer for even cooking.

   b. Air fry for 12 minutes, shaking the basket halfway through, until the mushrooms are golden brown and tender.

4. **Serve:** Transfer the air-fried mushrooms to a serving dish. If desired, garnish with fresh parsley before serving.

5. **Optional Serving Suggestion:** Serve as a side dish with your favorite protein, or enjoy as a tasty appetizer.

Air-Fried Zucchini Fritters with Greek Yogurt

Yield: *4 servings (12 fritters)* | Prep Time: *20 minutes* | Cook Time: *10 minutes*

INGREDIENTS:

2 medium zucchinis, grated

1 teaspoon salt (for draining zucchini)

1/2 cup feta cheese, crumbled

1/4 cup fresh dill, chopped

1/4 cup scallions, chopped

1/2 cup all-purpose flour

1 teaspoon baking powder

1/2 teaspoon black pepper

2 large eggs, beaten

Olive oil spray (for air frying)

Greek yogurt or tzatziki, for serving

NUTRITIONAL INFORMATION
(per serving, 3 fritters):

Calories: 180 • **Total Fat:** 8g • **Saturated Fat:** 3g • **Cholesterol:** 95mg • **Sodium:** 400mg • **Total Carbohydrates:** 18g • **Dietary Fiber:** 2g • **Sugars:** 3g • **Protein:** 9g

DIRECTIONS:

1. **Drain the Zucchini:** Place the grated zucchini in a colander and sprinkle with 1 teaspoon of salt. Let it sit for 10 minutes to draw out moisture. Squeeze the zucchini to remove as much water as possible.

2. **Mix the Fritter Batter:** In a large bowl, combine the drained zucchini, crumbled feta cheese, chopped dill, chopped scallions, all-purpose flour, baking powder, black pepper, and beaten eggs. Stir until the mixture is well combined.

3. Form the mixture into small patties, about 2-3 inches in diameter.

4. Preheat the air fryer to 380°F (190°C).

5. **Cook the Fritters:**

   a. Spray the air fryer basket with olive oil spray. Place the fritters in the basket, making sure they don't touch. You may need to cook in batches.

   b. Spray the tops of the fritters lightly with olive oil. Air fry for 10 minutes, flipping halfway through, until they are golden brown and crispy.

6. Serve the Greek-style zucchini fritters hot with Greek yogurt or tzatziki sauce on the side.

Air-Fried Broccoli with Garlic and Parmesan

Yield: *4 servings* | Prep Time: *10 minutes* | Cook Time: *10 minutes*

INGREDIENTS:

1 pound broccoli florets

2 tablespoons olive oil

3 cloves garlic, minced

1/4 cup grated Parmesan cheese

Salt and pepper to taste

Optional: Red pepper flakes for a spicy kick

Lemon wedges for serving

NUTRITIONAL INFORMATION
(per serving):

Calories: 120 • **Total Fat:** 8g • **Saturated Fat:** 2g • **Cholesterol:** 4mg • **Sodium:** 150mg • **Total Carbohydrates:** 8g • **Dietary Fiber:** 3g • **Sugars:** 2g • **Protein:** 5g

DIRECTIONS:

1. **Prep the Broccoli:** Wash the broccoli florets and pat them dry with paper towels. It's important to remove as much moisture as possible to ensure they become crispy when air-fried.

2. **Season the Broccoli:** In a large bowl, toss the broccoli florets with olive oil, minced garlic, salt, pepper, and optional red pepper flakes until well coated.

3. Preheat the air fryer to 400°F (200°C).

4. **Air Fry the Broccoli:**

   a. Transfer the seasoned broccoli to the air fryer basket, spreading them out into a single layer for even cooking. Depending on the size of your air fryer, you may need to cook the broccoli in batches.

   b. Air fry for 8-10 minutes, shaking the basket halfway through, until the broccoli is crispy and slightly golden.

5. **Add Parmesan:** Once cooked, transfer the broccoli to a serving bowl. While still hot, sprinkle the grated Parmesan cheese over the broccoli, tossing gently to evenly coat.

6. Serve the air-fried broccoli immediately, accompanied by lemon wedges, for a fresh burst of flavor.

Balsamic Glazed Air-Fried Beets

Yield: *4 servings* | Prep Time: *15 minutes* | Cook Time: *20 minutes*

INGREDIENTS:

4 medium beets, peeled and cut into 1/2-inch cubes

2 tablespoons olive oil

Salt and pepper to taste

1/4 cup balsamic vinegar

1 tablespoon honey

Optional: Fresh thyme or rosemary for garnish

DIRECTIONS:

1. **Prep the Beets:** After peeling and cubing the beets, toss them in a bowl with olive oil, salt, and pepper until evenly coated.

2. Preheat the air fryer to 380°F (190°C).

3. **Air Fry the Beets:**

   a. Transfer the seasoned beets to the air fryer basket, spreading them out into a single layer for even cooking. You may need to cook in batches depending on the size of your air fryer.

   b. Air fry for 18-20 minutes, shaking the basket halfway through the cooking time, until the beets are tender and slightly caramelized on the edges.

4. **Prepare the Balsamic Glaze:** While the beets are cooking, pour the balsamic vinegar and honey into a small saucepan. Bring to a simmer over medium heat, and reduce the mixture by half, about 5-7 minutes, until it thickens into a glaze. Remove from heat and let cool slightly; it will thicken further upon cooling.

5. **Serve:** Once the beets are cooked, transfer them to a serving dish. Drizzle the balsamic glaze over the beets and toss gently to coat. Garnish with fresh thyme or rosemary if desired before serving.

NUTRITIONAL INFORMATION
(per serving):

Calories: 150 • **Total Fat:** 7g • **Saturated Fat:** 1g • **Cholesterol:** 0mg • **Sodium:** 200mg • **Total Carbohydrates:** 20g • **Dietary Fiber:** 3g • **Sugars:** 17g (includes added sugars from honey) • **Protein:** 2g

Smokey Air-Fried Paprika Potatoes

Yield: *4 servings* | Prep Time: *15 minutes* | Cook Time: *20 minutes*

INGREDIENTS:

1.5 pounds baby potatoes, halved or quartered depending on size

2 tablespoons olive oil

1.5 teaspoons smoked paprika

1 teaspoon garlic powder

1/2 teaspoon onion powder

Salt and pepper to taste

Fresh parsley, chopped for garnish

DIRECTIONS:

1. **Prep the Potatoes:** Wash the baby potatoes and cut them into halves or quarters to ensure they cook evenly. Pat them dry with paper towels.

2. **Season the Potatoes:** In a large bowl, toss the potatoes with olive oil, smoked paprika, garlic powder, onion powder, salt, and pepper until well coated.

3. Preheat the air fryer to 400°F (200°C).

4. **Air Fry the Potatoes:**

   a. Arrange the seasoned potatoes in the air fryer basket in a single layer, ensuring they are not overcrowded. You may need to cook in batches depending on the size of your air fryer.

   b. Air fry for 20 minutes, shaking the basket halfway through the cooking time, until the potatoes are crispy on the outside and tender on the inside.

5. **Serve:** Transfer the air-fried potatoes to a serving dish. Garnish with chopped fresh parsley before serving.

NUTRITIONAL INFORMATION
(per serving):

Calories: 190 • **Total Fat:** 7g • **Saturated Fat:** 1g • **Cholesterol:** 0mg • **Sodium:** 10mg • **Total Carbohydrates:** 29g • **Dietary Fiber:** 4g • **Sugars:** 2g • **Protein:** 4g

Crispy Air-Fried Okra with Yogurt Dipping Sauce

Yield: *4 servings* | Prep Time: *15 minutes* | Cook Time: *12 minutes*

INGREDIENTS:

For Air-Fried Okra:

1 pound fresh okra, ends trimmed and cut into 1/2-inch pieces

1 tablespoon olive oil

1/2 cup cornmeal

1/2 teaspoon smoked paprika

1/2 teaspoon garlic powder

Salt and pepper to taste

For Yogurt Dipping Sauce:

1 cup plain Greek yogurt

1 tablespoon lemon juice

1 clove garlic, minced

1 tablespoon fresh dill, chopped (or 1 teaspoon dried dill)

Salt and pepper to taste

NUTRITIONAL INFORMATION (per serving):

Calories: 180 • Total Fat: 5g • Saturated Fat: 1g • Cholesterol: 3mg • Sodium: 150mg • Total Carbohydrates: 27g • Dietary Fiber: 5g • Sugars: 6g • Protein: 9g

DIRECTIONS:

1. **Prepare the Okra:**

   a. In a large bowl, toss the okra pieces with olive oil until well coated.

   b. In a separate bowl, mix together the cornmeal, smoked paprika, garlic powder, salt, and pepper.

   c. Add the okra to the cornmeal mixture and toss until evenly coated.

2. Preheat the air fryer to 390°F (200°C).

3. **Air Fry the Okra:**

   a. Place the coated okra pieces in the air fryer basket in a single layer, making sure they do not touch. You may need to cook in batches depending on the size of your air fryer.

   b. Air fry for 12 minutes, shaking the basket halfway through, until the okra is crispy and golden brown.

4. **Prepare the Yogurt Dipping Sauce:** While the okra is cooking, prepare the dipping sauce. In a small bowl, whisk together Greek yogurt, lemon juice, minced garlic, chopped dill, salt, and pepper until smooth. Adjust seasoning to taste.

5. Serve the crispy air-fried okra hot with the yogurt dipping sauce on the side.

Crispy Air-Fried Artichokes with Lemon Aioli

Yield: *4 servings* | Prep Time: *15 minutes* | Cook Time: *15 minutes*

INGREDIENTS:

For Air-Fried Artichokes:

2 cans (14 oz each) of artichoke hearts, drained and quartered

2 tablespoons olive oil

1 teaspoon garlic powder

1/2 teaspoon smoked paprika

Salt and pepper to taste

For Lemon Aioli:

1/2 cup mayonnaise

1 clove garlic, minced

2 tablespoons lemon juice

1 teaspoon lemon zest

Salt and pepper to taste

DIRECTIONS:

1. **Prepare the Artichokes:**

   a. Pat the artichoke hearts dry with paper towels to remove excess moisture. This will help them crisp up in the air fryer.

   b. In a bowl, toss the artichoke hearts with olive oil, garlic powder, smoked paprika, salt, and pepper until evenly coated.

2. Preheat the air fryer to 380°F (190°C).

3. **Air Fry the Artichokes:**

   a. Arrange the seasoned artichoke hearts in the air fryer basket in a single layer, ensuring they don't overlap. You may need to cook in batches depending on the size of your air fryer.

   b. Air fry for 15 minutes, shaking the basket halfway through, until the artichokes are golden and crispy.

NUTRITIONAL INFORMATION
(per Florentine, approximate):

Calories: 290 • **Total Fat:** 25g • **Saturated Fat:**
4g • **Cholesterol:** 15mg • **Sodium:** 480mg • **Total
Carbohydrates:** 15g • **Dietary Fiber:** 7g • **Sugars:**
2g • **Protein:** 4g

4. **Prepare the Lemon Aioli:** While the artichokes are cooking, prepare the aioli. In a small bowl, whisk together mayonnaise, minced garlic, lemon juice, lemon zest, salt, and pepper until smooth. Adjust the seasoning as needed.

5. Serve the crispy air-fried artichokes hot, accompanied by the lemon aioli for dipping.

Air-Fried Cauliflower Steaks with Tahini Drizzle

Yield: **4 servings** | Prep Time: **10 minutes** | Cook Time: **15 minutes**

INGREDIENTS:

For Cauliflower Steaks:
1 large head of cauliflower
2 tablespoons olive oil
1/2 teaspoon paprika
Salt and pepper to taste

For Tahini Drizzle:
1/4 cup tahini
2 tablespoons lemon juice
1 clove garlic, minced
2-4 tablespoons water (as needed for consistency)
Salt to taste
Optional: Fresh parsley, chopped for garnish
Optional: Sesame seeds for garnish

DIRECTIONS:

1. **Prepare the Cauliflower Steaks:**

   a. Remove the leaves from the cauliflower and trim the stem without removing it completely. Slice the cauliflower from top to base into 4 even steaks, approximately 3/4-inch thick. Reserve any leftover cauliflower for another use.

   b. Brush both sides of each cauliflower steak with olive oil and season with paprika, salt, and pepper.

2. Preheat the air fryer to 400°F (200°C).

3. **Air Fry the Cauliflower Steaks:**

   a. Place the cauliflower steaks in the air fryer basket in a single layer. You may need to work in batches depending on the size of your air fryer.

   b. Air fry for 12-15 minutes, flipping halfway through, until the cauliflower steaks are tender and golden brown on the edges.

4. **Prepare the Tahini Drizzle:** While the cauliflower is cooking, whisk together tahini, lemon juice, minced garlic, and salt in a small bowl. Gradually add water until you reach a drizzling consistency.

5. **Serve:** Arrange the air-fried cauliflower steaks on a serving platter. Drizzle with the tahini sauce and garnish with chopped parsley and sesame seeds if desired.

6. **Optional Serving Suggestion:** Serve with a side of quinoa or a fresh salad for a complete meal.

NUTRITIONAL INFORMATION
(per serving):

Calories: 180 • **Total Fat:** 14g • **Saturated Fat:**
2g • **Cholesterol:** 0mg • **Sodium:** 75mg • **Total
Carbohydrates:** 12g • **Dietary Fiber:** 4g • **Sugars:**
4g • **Protein:** 5g

Mediterranean Stuffed Bell Peppers with Quinoa

Yield: *4 servings* | Prep Time: *20 minutes* | Cook Time: *15 minutes*

INGREDIENTS:

4 large bell peppers, tops cut off and seeds removed

1 cup quinoa, cooked according to package instructions

1 tablespoon olive oil

1 small onion, finely chopped

2 cloves garlic, minced

1 cup cherry tomatoes, quartered

1/2 cup Kalamata olives, pitted and chopped

1/2 cup crumbled feta cheese

1/4 cup fresh parsley, chopped

1 teaspoon dried oregano

Salt and pepper to taste

1/4 cup water (for cooking)

Additional feta cheese and fresh parsley for garnish

NUTRITIONAL INFORMATION
(per serving):

Calories: 290 • Total Fat: 12g • Saturated Fat: 4g • Cholesterol: 20mg • Sodium: 400mg • Total Carbohydrates: 36g • Dietary Fiber: 6g • Sugars: 8g • Protein: 10g

DIRECTIONS:

1. **Prepare the Filling:**

   a. In a large skillet over medium heat, heat the olive oil. Add the onion and garlic, and sauté until softened, about 5 minutes.

   b. Stir in the cooked quinoa, cherry tomatoes, Kalamata olives, crumbled feta cheese, chopped parsley, dried oregano, salt, and pepper. Cook for an additional 2 minutes, stirring frequently. Remove from heat.

2. **Stuff the Bell Peppers:** Spoon the quinoa mixture into each bell pepper, pressing down gently to pack the filling.

3. Preheat the air fryer to 360°F (180°C).

4. **Air Fry the Stuffed Peppers:**

   a. Pour 1/4 cup water into the bottom of the air fryer basket or tray (to prevent the peppers from drying out). Place the stuffed bell peppers in the basket or tray.

   b. Air fry for 15 minutes or until the peppers are tender and the filling is heated through.

5. **Serve:** Carefully remove the stuffed bell peppers from the air fryer. Garnish with additional feta cheese and fresh parsley before serving.

Spicy Air-Fried Chickpeas with Harissa

Yield: *4 servings* | Prep Time: *5 minutes* | Cook Time: *15 minutes*

INGREDIENTS:

2 cans (15 oz each) chickpeas, drained, rinsed, and patted dry

2 tablespoons olive oil

2 tablespoons harissa paste

1 teaspoon ground cumin

Salt to taste

NUTRITIONAL INFORMATION
(per serving):

Calories: 240 • Total Fat: 10g • Saturated Fat: 1.5g • Cholesterol: 0mg • Sodium: 300mg (adjust based on salt added) • Total Carbohydrates: 30g • Dietary Fiber: 8g • Sugars: 6g • Protein: 10g

DIRECTIONS:

1. Preheat the air fryer to 390°F (200°C).

2. **Season the Chickpeas:** In a large bowl, combine the dried chickpeas, olive oil, harissa paste, ground cumin, and salt. Toss until the chickpeas are evenly coated with the seasoning.

3. **Air Fry the Chickpeas:**

   a. Transfer the seasoned chickpeas to the air fryer basket, spreading them out into a single layer for even cooking.

   b. Air fry for 15 minutes, shaking the basket every 5 minutes, until the chickpeas are crispy and golden.

4. Serve the spicy air-fried chickpeas warm or at room temperature as a snack or appetizer.

Chapter 5

Salads and Side Dishes

Mediterranean Air-Fried Vegetable Salad with Feta

Yield: *4 servings* | Prep Time: *15 minutes* | Cook Time: *20 minutes*

INGREDIENTS:

For the Salad:

1 zucchini, cut into 1/2-inch slices

1 yellow squash, cut into 1/2-inch slices

1 red bell pepper, cut into 1-inch pieces

1 yellow bell pepper, cut into 1-inch pieces

1 red onion, cut into wedges

2 tablespoons olive oil

1 teaspoon dried oregano

Salt and pepper to taste

1 cup cherry tomatoes, halved

1/2 cup Kalamata olives

1/2 cup crumbled feta cheese

1/4 cup fresh basil leaves, torn

For the Dressing:

3 tablespoons extra virgin olive oil

2 tablespoons red wine vinegar

1 teaspoon Dijon mustard

1 clove garlic, minced

Salt and pepper to taste

NUTRITIONAL INFORMATION
(per serving):

Calories: 290 • **Total Fat:** 23g • **Saturated Fat:** 6g • **Cholesterol:** 25mg • **Sodium:** 480mg • **Total Carbohydrates:** 16g • **Dietary Fiber:** 3g • **Sugars:** 9g • **Protein:** 6g

DIRECTIONS:

1. Preheat the air fryer to 400°F (200°C).

2. **Prepare the Vegetables:** In a large bowl, toss the zucchini, yellow squash, red bell pepper, yellow bell pepper, and red onion with 2 tablespoons olive oil, dried oregano, salt, and pepper until well coated.

3. **Air Fry the Vegetables:** Transfer the seasoned vegetables to the air fryer basket. Air fry for 15-20 minutes, shaking the basket halfway through, until the vegetables are tender and lightly charred. You may need to cook in batches depending on the size of your air fryer.

4. **Make the Dressing:** While the vegetables are cooking, whisk together the extra virgin olive oil, red wine vinegar, Dijon mustard, minced garlic, salt, and pepper in a small bowl. Set aside.

5. **Assemble the Salad:** In a large salad bowl, combine the air-fried vegetables, cherry tomatoes, and Kalamata olives. Drizzle with the prepared dressing and toss gently to combine.

6. **Serve:** Top the salad with crumbled feta cheese and torn basil leaves before serving.

Air-Fried Zucchini and Bell Pepper Salad with Lemon-Herb Dressing

Yield: *4 servings* | Prep Time: *15 minutes* | Cook Time: *10 minutes*

INGREDIENTS:

For Salad:

2 medium zucchinis, sliced into 1/4-inch rounds

1 red bell pepper, sliced into strips

1 yellow bell pepper, sliced into strips

1 tablespoon olive oil

Salt and pepper to taste

For Lemon-Herb Dressing:

3 tablespoons extra virgin olive oil

Juice of 1 lemon

1 clove garlic, minced

1 tablespoon fresh parsley, finely chopped

1 tablespoon fresh basil, finely chopped

Salt and pepper to taste

DIRECTIONS:

1. **Prepare the Vegetables:** Toss the sliced zucchinis and bell peppers with 1 tablespoon of olive oil, salt, and pepper until evenly coated.

2. **Air Fry the Vegetables:**

   a. Preheat the air fryer to 400°F (200°C).

   b. Arrange the vegetables in the air fryer basket in a single layer, working in batches if necessary to avoid overcrowding.

   c. Air fry for 8-10 minutes, or until the vegetables are tender and slightly charred, shaking the basket halfway through cooking.

NUTRITIONAL INFORMATION
(per serving):

Calories: 150 • Total Fat: 11g • Saturated Fat:
1.5g • Cholesterol: 0mg • Sodium: 75mg • Total
Carbohydrates: 12g • Dietary Fiber: 3g • Sugars:
6g • Protein: 2g

3. **Make the Lemon-Herb Dressing:** In a small bowl, whisk together the extra virgin olive oil, lemon juice, minced garlic, chopped parsley, chopped basil, salt, and pepper until well combined.

4. **Assemble the Salad:** Transfer the air-fried vegetables to a large salad bowl. Drizzle the lemon-herb dressing over the vegetables and toss gently to combine.

5. Serve the salad warm or at room temperature, garnished with additional fresh herbs if desired.

Roasted Cauliflower and Lentil Salad with Tahini Dressing

Yield: **4 servings** | Prep Time: **15 minutes** | Cook Time: **20 minutes**

INGREDIENTS:

For Salad:

1 large head of cauliflower, cut into florets
1 tablespoon olive oil
1/2 teaspoon smoked paprika
Salt and pepper to taste
1 cup green lentils, rinsed
2 cups vegetable broth or water
1/2 cup cherry tomatoes, halved
1/4 cup red onion, finely chopped
1/4 cup fresh parsley, chopped
1/4 cup walnuts, chopped (optional)

For Tahini Dressing:

1/4 cup tahini
2 tablespoons lemon juice
1 clove garlic, minced
2-4 tablespoons water (to thin)
Salt to taste

NUTRITIONAL INFORMATION
(per serving):

Calories: 320 • Total Fat: 14g • Saturated Fat:
2g • Cholesterol: 0mg • Sodium: 300mg • Total
Carbohydrates: 38g • Dietary Fiber: 16g • Sugars: 4g •
Protein: 15g

DIRECTIONS:

1. **Cook the Lentils:** In a medium saucepan, combine the lentils and vegetable broth (or water). Bring to a boil, then reduce heat to low, cover, and simmer for 15-20 minutes or until lentils are tender but not mushy. Drain any excess liquid and let cool.

2. **Prepare and Cook Cauliflower:** Toss cauliflower florets with olive oil, smoked paprika, salt, and pepper. Preheat the air fryer to 400°F (200°C). Arrange the cauliflower in the air fryer basket in a single layer (work in batches if necessary). Air fry for 15-20 minutes, shaking halfway through, until the cauliflower is tender and has crispy edges.

3. **Make the Tahini Dressing:** In a small bowl, whisk together tahini, lemon juice, minced garlic, and salt. Gradually add water until you reach the desired consistency for the dressing.

4. **Assemble the Salad:** In a large salad bowl, combine the cooled lentils, roasted cauliflower, cherry tomatoes, red onion, and chopped parsley. If using, add chopped walnuts.

5. Drizzle the tahini dressing over the salad and toss gently to combine.

6. Serve the salad immediately, or chill in the refrigerator for an hour to allow flavors to meld.

Greek Air-Fried Potato Salad with Olives and Feta

Yield: *4 servings* | Prep Time: *15 minutes* | Cook Time: *20 minutes*

INGREDIENTS:

For the Salad:

1.5 pounds baby potatoes, halved

2 tablespoons olive oil

1 teaspoon dried oregano

Salt and pepper to taste

1/2 cup Kalamata olives, pitted and halved

1/2 red onion, thinly sliced

1/2 cup cherry tomatoes, halved

1/2 cup cucumber, diced

1/2 cup feta cheese, crumbled

2 tablespoons fresh parsley, chopped

For the Dressing:

3 tablespoons extra virgin olive oil

2 tablespoons red wine vinegar

1 clove garlic, minced

1 teaspoon Dijon mustard

Salt and pepper to taste

NUTRITIONAL INFORMATION (per serving):

Calories: 350 • Total Fat: 22g • Saturated Fat: 5g • Cholesterol: 20mg • Sodium: 450mg • Total Carbohydrates: 31g • Dietary Fiber: 4g • Sugars: 4g • Protein: 7g

DIRECTIONS:

1. **Cook the Potatoes:**

   a. Toss the halved baby potatoes with 2 tablespoons of olive oil, dried oregano, salt, and pepper until evenly coated.

   b. Preheat the air fryer to 400°F (200°C).

   c. Arrange the potatoes in the air fryer basket in a single layer. You may need to work in batches depending on the size of your air fryer.

   d. Air fry for 20 minutes, shaking halfway through, until the potatoes are golden brown and fork-tender. Let cool slightly.

2. **Prepare the Dressing:** In a small bowl, whisk together the extra virgin olive oil, red wine vinegar, minced garlic, Dijon mustard, salt, and pepper. Set aside.

3. **Assemble the Salad:**

   a. In a large salad bowl, combine the air-fried potatoes, Kalamata olives, red onion, cherry tomatoes, cucumber, and feta cheese.

   b. Drizzle the dressing over the salad and toss gently to combine.

4. **Serve:** Garnish the salad with fresh parsley before serving. Serve warm or at room temperature.

Air-Fried Brussels Sprouts Caesar Salad

Yield: *4 servings* | Prep Time: *15 minutes* | Cook Time: *12 minutes*

INGREDIENTS:

For the Salad:

1 pound Brussels sprouts, trimmed and halved

2 tablespoons olive oil

Salt and pepper to taste

1/4 cup grated Parmesan cheese

2 cups romaine lettuce, chopped

1/4 cup croutons

For the Caesar Dressing:

1/2 cup mayonnaise

2 cloves garlic, minced

2 tablespoons lemon juice

1 tablespoon Worcestershire sauce

1 teaspoon Dijon mustard

1/4 cup grated Parmesan cheese

Salt and pepper to taste

2 tablespoons water (optional, to thin)

DIRECTIONS:

1. **Air Fry the Brussels Sprouts:**

   a. Toss the Brussels sprouts with olive oil, salt, and pepper until well coated.

   b. Preheat the air fryer to 400°F (200°C).

   c. Arrange the Brussels sprouts in the air fryer basket, cut side down, in a single layer. You may need to work in batches.

   d. Air fry for 10-12 minutes or until the Brussels sprouts are crispy and golden. Shake the basket halfway through cooking.

2. **Prepare the Caesar Dressing:** In a bowl, whisk together mayonnaise, minced garlic, lemon juice, Worcestershire sauce, Dijon mustard, and grated Parmesan. Season with salt and pepper to taste. If the dressing is too thick, whisk in water 1 tablespoon at a time until reaching the desired consistency.

3. **Assemble the Salad:**

   a. In a large salad bowl, combine the air-fried Brussels sprouts, chopped romaine lettuce, and croutons.

   b. Drizzle the Caesar dressing over the salad and toss to combine. Ensure all components are evenly coated.

4. **Serve:** Sprinkle the salad with additional grated Parmesan cheese before serving.

NUTRITIONAL INFORMATION
(per serving):

Calories: 330 • **Total Fat:** 28g • **Saturated Fat:** 5g • **Cholesterol:** 25mg • **Sodium:** 550mg • **Total Carbohydrates:** 15g • **Dietary Fiber:** 4g • **Sugars:** 4g • **Protein:** 8g

Crispy Chickpea and Quinoa Tabbouleh Salad

Yield: *4 servings* | Prep Time: *20 minutes* | Cook Time: *15 minutes*

INGREDIENTS:

For the Crispy Chickpeas:

1 can (15 oz) chickpeas, drained, rinsed, and patted dry

1 tablespoon olive oil

1/2 teaspoon paprika

Salt and pepper to taste

For the Quinoa Tabbouleh:

1 cup quinoa, rinsed

2 cups water

1 cup fresh parsley, finely chopped

1/2 cup fresh mint, finely chopped

2 tomatoes, diced

1 cucumber, diced

1/4 cup red onion, finely chopped

Juice of 2 lemons

3 tablespoons olive oil

Salt and pepper to taste

DIRECTIONS:

1. **Cook the Quinoa:** In a medium saucepan, bring 2 cups of water to a boil. Add the quinoa and reduce the heat to low. Cover and simmer for 15 minutes or until all water is absorbed. Remove from heat and let it sit covered for 5 minutes. Fluff with a fork and let it cool.

2. **Prepare the Crispy Chickpeas:**

   a. Preheat the air fryer to 390°F (200°C).

   b. Toss the chickpeas with 1 tablespoon olive oil, paprika, salt, and pepper. Spread them in a single layer in the air fryer basket.

   c. Air fry for 12-15 minutes, shaking the basket halfway through until the chickpeas are golden and crispy. Let them cool.

3. **Make the Tabbouleh:**

   a. In a large bowl, combine the cooled quinoa, parsley, mint, tomatoes, cucumber, and red onion.

   b. In a small bowl, whisk together lemon juice, 3 tablespoons of olive oil, salt, and pepper. Pour the dressing over the quinoa mixture and toss to combine.

4. **Assemble the Salad:** Just before serving, fold the crispy chickpeas into the quinoa tabbouleh.

5. Serve the salad immediately to maintain the crispiness of the chickpeas, garnished with extra herbs if desired.

NUTRITIONAL INFORMATION
(per serving):

Calories: 400 • **Total Fat:** 18g • **Saturated Fat:** 2.5g • **Cholesterol:** 0mg • **Sodium:** 300mg • **Total Carbohydrates:** 50g • **Dietary Fiber:** 10g • **Sugars:** 5g • **Protein:** 14g

Air-Fried Herbed Baby Potatoes

Yield: *4 servings* │ Prep Time: *10 minutes* │ Cook Time: *20 minutes*

INGREDIENTS:

1.5 pounds baby potatoes, halved or quartered depending on size

2 tablespoons olive oil

1 teaspoon dried rosemary

1 teaspoon dried thyme

1/2 teaspoon garlic powder

Salt and pepper to taste

Fresh parsley, chopped for garnish (optional)

NUTRITIONAL INFORMATION (per serving):

Calories: 220 • **Total Fat:** 7g • **Saturated Fat:** 1g • **Cholesterol:** 0mg • **Sodium:** 10mg • **Total Carbohydrates:** 37g • **Dietary Fiber:** 5g • **Sugars:** 2g • **Protein:** 4g

DIRECTIONS:

1. **Prep the Potatoes:** Wash the baby potatoes and cut them into halves or quarters to ensure they cook evenly.

2. **Season the Potatoes:** In a large bowl, toss the potatoes with olive oil, dried rosemary, dried thyme, garlic powder, salt, and pepper until they are evenly coated.

3. Preheat the air fryer to 400°F (200°C).

4. **Air Fry the Potatoes:**

   a. Arrange the seasoned potatoes in the air fryer basket in a single layer, ensuring there's a little space between them for even cooking. You may need to cook in batches depending on the size of your air fryer.

   b. Air fry for 20 minutes, shaking the basket halfway through, or until the potatoes are golden brown and crispy on the outside and tender on the inside.

5. **Serve:** Transfer the air-fried herbed baby potatoes to a serving dish. If desired, garnish with fresh parsley before serving.

Air-Fried Garlic and Parmesan Eggplant Slices

Yield: *4 servings* │ Prep Time: *15 minutes (plus 30 minutes for salting)* │ Cook Time: *10 minutes*

INGREDIENTS:

1 large eggplant, sliced into 1/2-inch thick rounds

1 teaspoon salt (for drawing out moisture from eggplant)

2 tablespoons olive oil

2 cloves garlic, minced

1/2 cup grated Parmesan cheese

1 teaspoon dried oregano

1/2 teaspoon black pepper

Fresh parsley, chopped for garnish (optional)

NUTRITIONAL INFORMATION (per serving):

Calories: 150 • **Total Fat:** 10g • **Saturated Fat:** 3g • **Cholesterol:** 11mg • **Sodium:** 630mg • **Total Carbohydrates:** 9g • **Dietary Fiber:** 4g • **Sugars:** 4g • **Protein:** 7g

DIRECTIONS:

1. **Salt the Eggplant:** Arrange the eggplant slices in a single layer on paper towels and sprinkle both sides with salt. Let them sit for 30 minutes to draw out moisture. Pat the slices dry with paper towels to remove excess moisture and salt.

2. **Season the Eggplant:** In a small bowl, mix together the olive oil and minced garlic. Brush both sides of the eggplant slices with the garlic-infused olive oil. Sprinkle the grated Parmesan cheese, dried oregano, and black pepper evenly over the slices.

3. Preheat the air fryer to 380°F (190°C).

4. **Air Fry the Eggplant:**

   a. Arrange the eggplant slices in the air fryer basket in a single layer. You may need to work in batches depending on the size of your air fryer.

   b. Air fry for 10 minutes, flipping the slices halfway through or until the eggplant is tender and the cheese is golden and crispy.

5. Serve the air-fried eggplant slices hot, garnished with chopped fresh parsley if desired.

Spicy Air-Fried Olives Stuffed with Almonds

Yield: *4 servings* | Prep Time: *15 minutes* | Cook Time: *8 minutes*

INGREDIENTS:

1 cup large green olives, pitted

1/4 cup whole almonds

1 tablespoon olive oil

1/2 teaspoon smoked paprika

1/4 teaspoon red pepper flakes (adjust to taste)

1/4 teaspoon garlic powder

Salt (optional, as olives may already be salty)

NUTRITIONAL INFORMATION (per serving):

Calories: 120 • **Total Fat:** 11g • **Saturated Fat:** 1.5g • **Cholesterol:** 0mg • **Sodium:** 300mg (varies based on olive salt content) • **Total Carbohydrates:** 4g • **Dietary Fiber:** 2g • **Sugars:** 0g • **Protein:** 2g

DIRECTIONS:

1. **Prep the Olives:** Carefully insert a whole almond into the cavity of each olive where the pit was removed. This can be a bit delicate, so take your time to avoid splitting the olives.

2. **Season the Olives:** In a bowl, mix together olive oil, smoked paprika, red pepper flakes, garlic powder, and a pinch of salt (if using). Toss the stuffed olives in the spice mix until they are evenly coated.

3. Preheat the air fryer to 380°F (190°C).

4. **Air Fry the Olives:**

   a. Arrange the stuffed olives in the air fryer basket in a single layer, ensuring they are not touching. You may need to cook in batches depending on the size of your air fryer.

   b. Air fry for 6-8 minutes or until the olives are heated through and slightly crispy on the outside.

5. Serve the spicy air-fried olives warm as a unique appetizer or snack.

Air-Fried Greek Lemon Garlic Potatoes

Yield: *4 servings* | Prep Time: *15 minutes* | Cook Time: *20 minutes*

INGREDIENTS:

1.5 pounds baby potatoes, halved or quartered depending on size

3 tablespoons olive oil

Juice of 1 lemon

2 cloves garlic, minced

1 teaspoon dried oregano

1/2 teaspoon dried thyme

Salt and pepper to taste

Fresh parsley, chopped for garnish

Lemon wedges for serving

NUTRITIONAL INFORMATION (per serving):

Calories: 220 • **Total Fat:** 11g • **Saturated Fat:** 1.5g • **Cholesterol:** 0mg • **Sodium:** 300mg • **Total Carbohydrates:** 29g • **Dietary Fiber:** 4g • **Sugars:** 2g • **Protein:** 3g

DIRECTIONS:

1. **Prepare the Potatoes:** Wash the baby potatoes and cut them into halves or quarters to ensure they cook evenly. Pat them dry with paper towels.

2. **Season the Potatoes:** In a large bowl, mix together the olive oil, lemon juice, minced garlic, dried oregano, dried thyme, salt, and pepper. Add the potatoes to the bowl and toss until they are well coated with the seasoning mix.

3. Preheat the air fryer to 400°F (200°C).

4. **Air Fry the Potatoes:**

   a. Arrange the seasoned potatoes in the air fryer basket in a single layer, ensuring there's a little space between them for even cooking. You may need to cook in batches depending on the size of your air fryer.

   b. Air fry for 20 minutes, shaking the basket halfway through, or until the potatoes are golden brown and crispy on the outside and tender on the inside.

5. **Serve:** Transfer the air-fried potatoes to a serving dish. Garnish with fresh parsley and serve with lemon wedges on the side.

Air-Fried Tomato and Feta Bruschetta

Yield: *4 servings* | Prep Time: *15 minutes* | Cook Time: *5 minutes*

INGREDIENTS:

1 baguette, sliced into 1/2-inch thick rounds

2 tablespoons olive oil

2 cups cherry tomatoes, halved

1/2 cup feta cheese, crumbled

1/4 cup fresh basil leaves, chopped

2 cloves garlic, minced

Salt and pepper to taste

Balsamic glaze for drizzling (optional)

NUTRITIONAL INFORMATION (per serving):

Calories: 220 • **Total Fat:** 9g • **Saturated Fat:** 3g • **Cholesterol:** 15mg • **Sodium:** 480mg • **Total Carbohydrates:** 28g • **Dietary Fiber:** 2g • **Sugars:** 4g • **Protein:** 8g

DIRECTIONS:

1. **Prep the Baguette:** Brush both sides of each baguette slice with olive oil. Set aside.

2. **Make the Tomato-Feta Topping:** In a bowl, combine the halved cherry tomatoes, crumbled feta cheese, chopped basil, minced garlic, and a pinch of salt and pepper. Toss gently to mix.

3. Preheat the air fryer to 350°F (180°C).

4. **Air Fry the Baguette Slices:**

   a. Arrange the oiled baguette slices in the air fryer basket in a single layer. You may need to work in batches depending on the size of your air fryer.

   b. Air fry for 3-5 minutes or until the baguette slices are golden and crispy. Remove and let cool slightly.

5. **Assemble the Bruschetta:** Spoon the tomato-feta mixture generously onto each toasted baguette slice.

6. **Serve:** Arrange the bruschetta on a serving platter. Drizzle with balsamic glaze if desired, and serve immediately.

Air-Fried Carrots with Honey and Dill

Yield: *4 servings* | Prep Time: *10 minutes* | Cook Time: *15 minutes*

INGREDIENTS:

1 pound carrots, peeled and cut into sticks

2 tablespoons olive oil

2 tablespoons honey

1 tablespoon fresh dill, chopped (or 1 teaspoon dried dill)

Salt and pepper to taste

NUTRITIONAL INFORMATION (per serving):

Calories: 140 • **Total Fat:** 7g • **Saturated Fat:** 1g • **Cholesterol:** 0mg • **Sodium:** 85mg • **Total Carbohydrates:** 20g • **Dietary Fiber:** 3g • **Sugars:** 14g (includes 9g added sugars from honey) • **Protein:** 1g

DIRECTIONS:

1. **Prepare the Carrots:** Peel the carrots and cut them into sticks, approximately 3-4 inches long and 1/2 inch thick.

2. **Season the Carrots:** In a large bowl, toss the carrot sticks with olive oil, honey, and a pinch of salt and pepper until they are well coated.

3. Preheat the air fryer to 380°F (190°C).

4. **Air Fry the Carrots:**

   a. Arrange the carrot sticks in the air fryer basket in a single layer, ensuring there's a little space between them for even cooking. You may need to cook in batches depending on the size of your air fryer.

   b. Air fry for 15 minutes, shaking the basket halfway through or until the carrots are tender and caramelized at the edges.

5. **Serve:**

   a. Transfer the air-fried carrots to a serving dish. Sprinkle with chopped fresh dill, and toss gently to combine.

   b. Serve immediately as a delicious and healthy side dish.

Air-Fried Asparagus with Lemon and Parmesan

Yield: *4 servings* | Prep Time: *10 minutes* | Cook Time: *8 minutes*

INGREDIENTS:

1 pound fresh asparagus, tough ends trimmed

2 tablespoons olive oil

Salt and pepper to taste

Zest of 1 lemon

2 tablespoons lemon juice

1/4 cup grated Parmesan cheese

Additional lemon wedges for serving

NUTRITIONAL INFORMATION (per serving):

Calories: 110 • **Total Fat:** 8g • **Saturated Fat:** 2g • **Cholesterol:** 4mg • **Sodium:** 125mg • **Total Carbohydrates:** 6g • **Dietary Fiber:** 3g • **Sugars:** 2g • **Protein:** 5g

DIRECTIONS:

1. **Prep the Asparagus:** Rinse the asparagus and trim off the tough ends. Pat the asparagus dry with paper towels to remove any excess moisture.

2. **Season the Asparagus:** In a large bowl, toss the asparagus with olive oil, salt, and pepper until the spears are evenly coated.

3. Preheat the air fryer to 400°F (200°C).

4. **Air Fry the Asparagus:**

   a. Arrange the asparagus in the air fryer basket in a single layer. Depending on the size of your air fryer, you may need to cook in batches.

   b. Air fry for 7-8 minutes or until the asparagus is tender and slightly crispy at the tips. The cooking time may vary depending on the thickness of the asparagus spears.

5. **Add Lemon and Parmesan:** Once cooked, transfer the asparagus to a serving platter. Immediately sprinkle with lemon zest, lemon juice, and grated Parmesan cheese. Toss gently to combine.

6. Serve the asparagus immediately, garnished with additional lemon wedges on the side.

Turkish Spiced Air-Fried Cauliflower

Yield: *4 servings* | Prep Time: *10 minutes* | Cook Time: *15 minutes*

INGREDIENTS:

1 large head of cauliflower, cut into florets

2 tablespoons olive oil

1 teaspoon ground cumin

1 teaspoon smoked paprika

1/2 teaspoon ground turmeric

1/4 teaspoon ground cinnamon

1/4 teaspoon cayenne pepper (adjust according to heat preference)

Salt to taste

Fresh parsley, chopped for garnish

Lemon wedges for serving

NUTRITIONAL INFORMATION (per serving):

Calories: 120 • **Total Fat:** 7g • **Saturated Fat:** 1g • **Cholesterol:** 0mg • **Sodium:** 60mg • **Total Carbohydrates:** 13g • **Dietary Fiber:** 5g • **Sugars:** 5g • **Protein:** 4g

DIRECTIONS:

1. **Prepare the Cauliflower:** Wash the cauliflower and cut it into florets. Pat dry with paper towels to remove any excess moisture.

2. **Season the Cauliflower:** In a large bowl, combine the cauliflower florets with olive oil, ensuring they are evenly coated. Sprinkle the ground cumin, smoked paprika, ground turmeric, ground cinnamon, cayenne pepper, and salt over the cauliflower. Toss until the florets are well coated with the spices.

3. Preheat the air fryer to 390°F (200°C).

4. **Air Fry the Cauliflower:**

   a. Arrange the seasoned cauliflower florets in the air fryer basket in a single layer. Depending on the size of your air fryer, you may need to cook them in batches to avoid overcrowding.

   b. Air fry for 15 minutes, shaking the basket halfway through the cooking time, until the cauliflower is tender and has crispy edges.

5. **Serve:** Transfer the air-fried cauliflower to a serving dish. Garnish with fresh parsley and serve with lemon wedges on the side.

Air-Fried Beetroot and Goat Cheese Salad

Yield: *4 servings* | Prep Time: *15 minutes* | Cook Time: *20 minutes*

INGREDIENTS:

For the Salad:

4 medium beetroots, peeled and cut into 1/2-inch cubes

2 tablespoons olive oil

Salt and pepper to taste

4 cups mixed salad greens (such as arugula, spinach, and baby kale)

1/2 cup walnuts, roughly chopped

1/2 cup goat cheese, crumbled

1/4 cup red onion, thinly sliced

For the Dressing:

3 tablespoons extra virgin olive oil

2 tablespoons balsamic vinegar

1 teaspoon Dijon mustard

1 teaspoon honey

Salt and pepper to taste

NUTRITIONAL INFORMATION (per serving):

Calories: 320 • **Total Fat:** 24g • **Saturated Fat:** 6g • **Cholesterol:** 13mg • **Sodium:** 220mg • **Total Carbohydrates:** 20g • **Dietary Fiber:** 5g • **Sugars:** 13g • **Protein:** 8g

DIRECTIONS:

1. **Prepare the Beetroots:** Toss the beetroot cubes with 2 tablespoons of olive oil, salt, and pepper until well coated.

2. **Air Fry the Beetroots:**

   a. Preheat the air fryer to 400°F (200°C).

   b. Arrange the beetroot cubes in the air fryer basket in a single layer. You may need to cook in batches depending on the size of your air fryer.

   c. Air fry for 20 minutes, shaking the basket halfway through until the beetroots are tender and slightly caramelized. Let cool slightly.

3. **Prepare the Dressing:** In a small bowl, whisk together the extra virgin olive oil, balsamic vinegar, Dijon mustard, honey, salt, and pepper. Adjust seasoning to taste.

4. **Assemble the Salad:**

   a. In a large salad bowl, combine the mixed salad greens, cooled beetroot cubes, walnuts, crumbled goat cheese, and red onion.

   b. Drizzle the dressing over the salad and gently toss to combine.

5. **Serve:** Divide the salad among plates and serve immediately.

Air-Fried Eggplant and Halloumi Cheese Salad

Yield: *4 servings* | Prep Time: *15 minutes* | Cook Time: *15 minutes*

INGREDIENTS:

For the Salad:

1 large eggplant, cut into 1/2-inch thick slices

8 ounces halloumi cheese, sliced

1 tablespoon olive oil

1 teaspoon dried oregano

Salt and pepper to taste

4 cups mixed salad greens (such as arugula, spinach, and romaine)

1/2 cup cherry tomatoes, halved

1/4 cup red onion, thinly sliced

1/4 cup Kalamata olives, pitted

For the Dressing:

3 tablespoons extra virgin olive oil

1 tablespoon balsamic vinegar

1 teaspoon Dijon mustard

1 clove garlic, minced

Salt and pepper to taste

DIRECTIONS:

1. Preheat the air fryer to 400°F (200°C).

2. **Prepare the Eggplant:**

   a. Brush both sides of the eggplant slices with 1 tablespoon olive oil and season with dried oregano, salt, and pepper.

   b. Place the eggplant slices in the air fryer basket in a single layer. You may need to work in batches.

   c. Air fry for 10-12 minutes, flipping halfway through, until the eggplant is tender and golden brown. Transfer to a plate and let cool.

3. **Cook the Halloumi:** Place the halloumi slices in the air fryer basket and cook for 2-3 minutes per side or until golden brown and slightly crispy. Remove and let cool slightly.

4. **Make the Dressing:** In a small bowl, whisk together the extra virgin olive oil, balsamic vinegar, Dijon mustard, minced garlic, salt, and pepper until well combined.

5. **Assemble the Salad:**

   a. In a large salad bowl, toss the mixed salad greens with cherry tomatoes, red onion, and Kalamata olives.

   b. Cut the air-fried eggplant and halloumi into bite-sized pieces and add them to the salad.

   c. Drizzle the dressing over the salad and gently toss to combine.

6. **Serve:** Divide the salad among plates and serve immediately.

NUTRITIONAL INFORMATION
(per serving):

Calories: 350 • **Total Fat:** 27g • **Saturated Fat:** 10g • **Cholesterol:** 35mg • **Sodium:** 800mg • **Total Carbohydrates:** 15g • **Dietary Fiber:** 5g • **Sugars:** 7g • **Protein:** 14g

Crispy Air-Fried Zucchini Fritters with Tzatziki

Yield: *4 servings* | Prep Time: *20 minutes* | Cook Time: *10 minutes*

INGREDIENTS:

For Zucchini Fritters:

2 medium zucchinis, grated

1 teaspoon salt (for drawing water out of zucchini)

1/2 cup all-purpose flour

1/4 cup grated Parmesan cheese

2 green onions, finely chopped

1 large egg, beaten

1 teaspoon garlic powder

1/2 teaspoon black pepper

1 tablespoon fresh dill, chopped (optional)

Olive oil spray for cooking

For Tzatziki:

1 cup Greek yogurt

1 small cucumber, grated and squeezed to remove excess water

2 cloves garlic, minced

2 tablespoons fresh dill, chopped

1 tablespoon olive oil

1 tablespoon lemon juice

Salt and pepper to taste

DIRECTIONS:

1. **Prepare the Zucchini:** Place the grated zucchini in a colander, sprinkle with 1 teaspoon salt, and let sit for 10 minutes to draw out moisture. Squeeze the zucchini to remove as much water as possible.

2. **Make Zucchini Fritter Mixture:** In a large bowl, combine the drained zucchini, flour, Parmesan cheese, green onions, beaten egg, garlic powder, black pepper, and chopped dill. Mix until well combined.

3. **Form the Fritters:** Shape the zucchini mixture into small patties about 1/2-inch thick.

4. Preheat the air fryer to 390°F (200°C). Spray the air fryer basket with olive oil spray to prevent sticking.

5. **Cook the Fritters:**

   a. Place the fritters in the air fryer basket in a single layer, working in batches if necessary. Spray the tops of the fritters with a little olive oil spray.

   b. Air fry for 10 minutes, flipping halfway through or until the fritters are golden and crispy.

6. **Prepare the Tzatziki:** While the fritters are cooking, prepare the tzatziki sauce by combining Greek yogurt, grated and squeezed cucumber, minced garlic, chopped dill, olive oil, lemon juice, salt, and pepper in a bowl. Mix until smooth.

7. Serve the crispy air-fried zucchini fritters hot with the tzatziki sauce on the side.

NUTRITIONAL INFORMATION
(per serving, including tzatziki):

Calories: 180 • **Total Fat:** 8g • **Saturated Fat:** 3g • **Cholesterol:** 55mg • **Sodium:** 630mg • **Total Carbohydrates:** 18g • **Dietary Fiber:** 2g • **Sugars:** 6g • **Protein:** 10g

Spicy Air-Fried Broccoli and Chickpea Salad

Yield: *4 servings* | Prep Time: *15 minutes* | Cook Time: *20 minutes*

INGREDIENTS:

For the Salad:

1 can (15 oz) chickpeas, drained, rinsed, and patted dry

1 large head of broccoli, cut into florets

2 tablespoons olive oil, divided

1/2 teaspoon smoked paprika

1/2 teaspoon chili powder

1/4 teaspoon cayenne pepper (adjust to taste)

Salt and pepper to taste

1/2 cup cherry tomatoes, halved

1/4 cup red onion, thinly sliced

1/4 cup feta cheese, crumbled

2 tablespoons fresh parsley, chopped

For the Dressing:

3 tablespoons extra virgin olive oil

1 tablespoon lemon juice

1 teaspoon honey

1 garlic clove, minced

Salt and pepper to taste

DIRECTIONS:

1. **Prepare the Chickpeas and Broccoli:**

   a. In a bowl, toss the chickpeas with 1 tablespoon of olive oil, smoked paprika, chili powder, cayenne pepper, and a pinch of salt and pepper.

   b. In another bowl, toss the broccoli florets with the remaining 1 tablespoon of olive oil and a pinch of salt and pepper.

2. **Air Fry the Chickpeas and Broccoli:**

   a. Preheat the air fryer to 400°F (200°C).

   b. Air fry the chickpeas for 10 minutes, shaking the basket halfway through.

   c. Remove the chickpeas and set aside. Next, air fry the broccoli for 10 minutes, until tender and the edges are crispy. You may need to do this in batches depending on the size of your air fryer.

3. **Prepare the Dressing:** In a small bowl, whisk together extra virgin olive oil, lemon juice, honey, minced garlic, salt, and pepper until emulsified.

4. **Assemble the Salad:**

   a. In a large salad bowl, combine the air-fried chickpeas, broccoli, cherry tomatoes, red onion, feta cheese, and parsley.

   b. Drizzle the dressing over the salad and gently toss to combine.

5. Serve the salad immediately, or chill in the refrigerator for about 30 minutes before serving for enhanced flavors.

NUTRITIONAL INFORMATION
(per serving):

Calories: 300 • Total Fat: 18g • Saturated Fat: 3g • Cholesterol: 8mg • Sodium: 300mg • Total Carbohydrates: 29g • Dietary Fiber: 8g • Sugars: 7g • Protein: 9g

Chapter 6

Fish and Seafood

Air-Fried Lemon Herb Salmon

Yield: *4 servings* | Prep Time: *10 minutes* | Cook Time: *10 minutes*

INGREDIENTS:

4 salmon fillets (about 6 ounces each)

2 tablespoons olive oil

1 lemon, zested and juiced

2 cloves garlic, minced

1 tablespoon fresh dill, chopped

1 tablespoon fresh parsley, chopped

Salt and pepper to taste

Additional lemon slices for serving

NUTRITIONAL INFORMATION
(per serving):

Calories: 280 • **Total Fat:** 17g •
Saturated Fat: 3g • **Cholesterol:**
75mg • **Sodium:** 100mg • **Total
Carbohydrates:** 1g • **Dietary Fiber:**
0g • **Sugars:** 0g • **Protein:** 29g

DIRECTIONS:

1. In a small bowl, mix together the olive oil, lemon zest, lemon juice, minced garlic, chopped dill, and parsley. Season with salt and pepper to taste.

2. Pat the salmon fillets dry with paper towels. Brush the lemon herb mixture generously over both sides of the salmon fillets.

3. Preheat the air fryer to 400°F (200°C).

4. Place the salmon fillets in the air fryer basket, skin-side down. Make sure they are not touching each other to allow for even cooking.

5. Air fry for 10 minutes, or until the salmon is cooked through and flakes easily with a fork. The exact cooking time may vary based on the thickness of the fillets.

6. Serve the air-fried lemon herb salmon hot, garnished with additional lemon slices.

Mediterranean Stuffed Sardines (Air Fryer Version)

Yield: *4 servings* | Prep Time: *20 minutes* | Cook Time: *10 minutes*

INGREDIENTS:

12 fresh sardines, cleaned and gutted

1/2 cup breadcrumbs

1/4 cup pine nuts, lightly toasted

1/4 cup raisins

2 tablespoons fresh parsley, chopped

1 clove garlic, minced

Zest of 1 lemon

2 tablespoons olive oil, plus extra for brushing

Salt and pepper to taste

Lemon wedges for serving

NUTRITIONAL INFORMATION
(per serving):

Calories: 280 • **Total Fat:** 15g •
Saturated Fat: 2g • **Cholesterol:**
85mg • **Sodium:** 350mg • **Total
Carbohydrates:** 20g • **Dietary Fiber:**
1g • **Sugars:** 8g • **Protein:** 20g

DIRECTIONS:

1. **Prepare the Stuffing:** In a bowl, combine the breadcrumbs, pine nuts, raisins, chopped parsley, minced garlic, lemon zest, and 1 tablespoon olive oil. Season with salt and pepper to taste. Mix well until the stuffing comes together.

2. **Stuff the Sardines:** Gently open each sardine and stuff with a small amount of the breadcrumb mixture. Close the sardines, pressing lightly to seal the stuffing inside.

3. Preheat the air fryer to 360°F (180°C).

4. **Prepare the Sardines for Air Frying:** Brush each stuffed sardine lightly with olive oil. This helps to crisp up the skin and prevents sticking.

5. **Air Fry the Sardines:**

   a. Arrange the stuffed sardines in the air fryer basket in a single layer. You may need to cook in batches depending on the size of your air fryer.

   b. Air fry for 10 minutes, flipping halfway through or until the sardines are golden and cooked through.

6. **Serve:** Carefully remove the sardines from the air fryer and place them on a serving platter. Serve immediately with lemon wedges on the side for squeezing over the sardines.

Greek-Style Air-Fried Cod with Olive Tapenade

Yield: *4 servings* | Prep Time: *15 minutes* | Cook Time: *12 minutes*

INGREDIENTS:

4 cod fillets (about 6 ounces each)

2 tablespoons olive oil

Salt and pepper to taste

1 lemon, sliced for garnish

For the Olive Tapenade:

1 cup Kalamata olives, pitted

1/4 cup capers, rinsed

2 cloves garlic, minced

2 tablespoons fresh parsley, chopped

1 tablespoon lemon juice

1/4 cup olive oil

Salt and pepper to taste

DIRECTIONS:

1. **Prepare the Olive Tapenade:**

   a. In a food processor, combine Kalamata olives, capers, garlic, parsley, and lemon juice. Pulse until the ingredients are finely chopped.

   b. With the processor running, slowly add 1/4 cup olive oil until the mixture is well combined but still has some texture. Season with salt and pepper to taste. Set aside.

2. **Prepare the Cod:** Pat the cod fillets dry with paper towels. Brush each fillet with olive oil and season with salt and pepper on both sides.

3. **Air Fry the Cod:**

   a. Preheat the air fryer to 400°F (200°C).

   b. Place the cod fillets in the air fryer basket, ensuring they don't overlap. You may need to cook in batches depending on the size of your air fryer.

   c. Air fry for 10-12 minutes, or until the cod flakes easily with a fork. The cooking time may vary based on the thickness of the fillets.

4. **Serve:** Plate the air-fried cod fillets and top each with a generous spoonful of the olive tapenade. Garnish with lemon slices.

NUTRITIONAL INFORMATION (per serving):

Calories: 320 • Total Fat: 22g • Saturated Fat: 3g • Cholesterol: 60mg • Sodium: 800mg • Total Carbohydrates: 4g • Dietary Fiber: 2g • Sugars: 0g • Protein: 27g

Air-Fried Squid with Lemon Aioli

Yield: *4 servings* | Prep Time: *15 minutes (plus 1 hour for marinating)* | Cook Time: *10 minutes*

INGREDIENTS:

For Squid:

1 pound squid, cleaned and cut into rings

2 tablespoons olive oil

1 teaspoon smoked paprika

Salt and pepper to taste

Lemon wedges for serving

For Lemon Aioli:

1/2 cup mayonnaise

1 clove garlic, minced

2 tablespoons lemon juice

1 teaspoon lemon zest

Salt to taste

DIRECTIONS:

1. **Marinate the Squid:** In a large bowl, combine the squid rings with olive oil, smoked paprika, salt, and pepper. Mix well to ensure the squid is evenly coated. Cover and refrigerate for at least 1 hour to marinate.

2. **Prepare the Lemon Aioli:** In a small bowl, whisk together mayonnaise, minced garlic, lemon juice, lemon zest, and salt until smooth. Refrigerate until ready to serve.

3. Preheat the air fryer to 400°F (200°C).

4. **Air Fry the Squid:**

   a. Arrange the marinated squid rings in the air fryer basket in a single layer, making sure they do not overlap. You may need to cook in batches depending on the size of your air fryer.

   b. Air fry for 8-10 minutes or until the squid is cooked through and slightly crispy. Shake the basket halfway through cooking to ensure even frying.

5. Serve the air-fried squid immediately with lemon aioli on the side for dipping and lemon wedges for added zest.

NUTRITIONAL INFORMATION (per serving):

Calories: 290 • Total Fat: 22g • Saturated Fat: 3g • Cholesterol: 265mg • Sodium: 300mg • Total Carbohydrates: 5g • Dietary Fiber: 0g • Sugars: 0g • Protein: 18g

Mediterranean Air-Fried Branzino with Capers

Yield: **2 servings** | Prep Time: **10 minutes** | Cook Time: **12 minutes**

INGREDIENTS:

2 whole branzino (sea bass), gutted and scaled, about 1 pound each

2 tablespoons olive oil

Salt and pepper to taste

2 lemons, 1 sliced and 1 for juice

4 sprigs fresh thyme

4 sprigs fresh rosemary

2 tablespoons capers, rinsed

2 cloves garlic, minced

Additional fresh herbs for garnish

NUTRITIONAL INFORMATION (per serving):

Calories: 440 • Total Fat: 28g • Saturated Fat: 4g • Cholesterol: 85mg • Sodium: 300mg • Total Carbohydrates: 6g • Dietary Fiber: 2g • Sugars: 1g • Protein: 40g

DIRECTIONS:

1. **Prepare the Branzino:**

   a. Rinse the branzino inside and out with cold water and pat dry with paper towels.

   b. Make 3-4 diagonal slashes on each side of the fish.

   c. Rub the outside of each fish with olive oil and season generously inside and out with salt and pepper.

   d. Stuff the cavity of each fish with lemon slices, thyme, and rosemary.

2. Preheat the air fryer to 390°F (200°C).

3. **Cook the Branzino:**

   a. Place the prepared branzino in the air fryer basket. Depending on the size of your air fryer, you may need to cook one fish at a time.

   b. Air fry for 12 minutes or until the fish is cooked through and the skin is crispy. There is no need to turn the fish during cooking.

4. **Make the Caper Garnish:** While the fish is cooking, mix the capers, minced garlic, and the juice of 1 lemon in a small bowl. Set aside.

5. **Serve:** Carefully remove the branzino from the air fryer and place on serving plates. Spoon the caper mixture over the fish. Garnish with additional fresh herbs.

Air-Fried Tuna Steaks with Lemon and Thyme

Yield: **2 servings** | Prep Time: **10 minutes (plus marinating time)** | Cook Time: **8 minutes**

INGREDIENTS:

2 tuna steaks (about 6 ounces each)

2 tablespoons olive oil

Juice and zest of 1 lemon

1 tablespoon fresh thyme leaves, finely chopped

2 cloves garlic, minced

Salt and pepper to taste

NUTRITIONAL INFORMATION (per serving):

Calories: 290 • Total Fat: 14g • Saturated Fat: 2g • Cholesterol: 65mg • Sodium: 150mg • Total Carbohydrates: 1g • Dietary Fiber: 0g • Sugars: 0g • Protein: 40g

DIRECTIONS:

1. **Marinate the Tuna Steaks:**

   a. In a small bowl, whisk together olive oil, lemon juice and zest, chopped thyme, minced garlic, salt, and pepper.

   b. Place the tuna steaks in a shallow dish or a resealable plastic bag. Pour the marinade over the tuna, ensuring each steak is well coated. Cover (or seal) and refrigerate for at least 30 minutes to 1 hour, turning the steaks halfway through the marinating time.

2. Preheat the air fryer to 400°F (200°C).

3. **Air Fry the Tuna Steaks:**

   a. Remove the tuna steaks from the marinade, letting excess drip off. Discard the remaining marinade.

   b. Place the tuna steaks in the air fryer basket, ensuring they are not touching.

   c. Air fry for 4 minutes. Flip the steaks and air fry for an additional 4 minutes for medium-rare or longer to your desired doneness.

4. **Serve:** Carefully remove the tuna steaks from the air fryer and let them rest for a few minutes. Serve the air-fried tuna steaks immediately, garnished with additional fresh thyme leaves and lemon wedges on the side.

Spicy Air-Fried Tilapia with Harissa Paste

Yield: *4 servings* | Prep Time: *10 minutes* | Cook Time: *12 minutes*

INGREDIENTS:

4 tilapia fillets (about 6 ounces each)

2 tablespoons harissa paste

1 tablespoon olive oil

1 teaspoon honey (optional, for balancing the heat)

Salt to taste

1 lemon, cut into wedges for serving

Fresh cilantro or parsley, chopped for garnish

NUTRITIONAL INFORMATION (per serving):

Calories: 180 • **Total Fat:** 6g • **Saturated Fat:** 1g • **Cholesterol:** 85mg • **Sodium:** 200mg (varies depending on the amount of salt and type of harissa paste used) • **Total Carbohydrates:** 2g • **Dietary Fiber:** 0g • **Sugars:** 1g (if honey is used) • **Protein:** 28g

DIRECTIONS:

1. **Marinate the Tilapia:**

   a. In a small bowl, mix together the harissa paste, olive oil, honey (if using), and a pinch of salt to create the marinade.

   b. Brush the marinade evenly over both sides of the tilapia fillets. Let them sit for about 10 minutes to absorb the flavors.

2. Preheat the air fryer to 400°F (200°C).

3. **Air Fry the Tilapia:**

   a. Place the marinated tilapia fillets in the air fryer basket, making sure they are not overlapping. Depending on the size of your air fryer, you may need to cook in batches.

   b. Air fry for 10-12 minutes or until the tilapia is cooked through and the exterior is slightly crisp. There's no need to flip the fillets during cooking.

4. **Serve:** Carefully remove the tilapia fillets from the air fryer and place them on serving plates. Garnish with chopped cilantro or parsley and serve with lemon wedges on the side.

Herb-Crusted Air-Fried Trout

Yield: *2 servings* | Prep Time: *15 minutes* | Cook Time: *10 minutes*

INGREDIENTS:

2 whole trout, gutted and scaled

1/4 cup fresh parsley, finely chopped

1/4 cup fresh dill, finely chopped

2 tablespoons fresh thyme leaves

2 cloves garlic, minced

1/4 cup breadcrumbs

2 tablespoons grated Parmesan cheese

2 tablespoons olive oil

Salt and pepper to taste

Lemon slices and additional herbs for serving

NUTRITIONAL INFORMATION (per serving):

Calories: 380 • **Total Fat:** 22g • **Saturated Fat:** 4g • **Cholesterol:** 105mg • **Sodium:** 350mg • **Total Carbohydrates:** 9g • **Dietary Fiber:** 1g • **Sugars:** 1g • **Protein:** 35g

DIRECTIONS:

1. **Prepare the Trout:** Rinse the trout under cold water and pat dry inside and out with paper towels. Season the inside of each trout with salt and pepper.

2. **Prepare the Herb Crust:** In a bowl, mix together the parsley, dill, thyme, minced garlic, breadcrumbs, grated Parmesan cheese, and 1 tablespoon of olive oil. Season with a pinch of salt and pepper. Mix until well combined.

3. **Crust the Trout:** Carefully press the herb mixture onto the outside of each trout, covering as much surface area as possible.

4. Preheat the air fryer to 400°F (200°C).

5. **Air Fry the Trout:**

   a. Brush the air fryer basket with the remaining 1 tablespoon of olive oil to prevent sticking.

   b. Place the herb-crusted trout in the air fryer basket. Depending on the size of your air fryer, you may need to cook one at a time.

   c. Air fry for 10 minutes, or until the trout is cooked through and the herb crust is golden and crispy.

6. **Serve:** Carefully remove the trout from the air fryer and transfer it to serving plates. Garnish with lemon slices and additional fresh herbs. Serve immediately.

Air-Fried Shrimp with Garlic and Parsley

Yield: *4 servings* | Prep Time: *10 minutes* | Cook Time: *8 minutes*

INGREDIENTS:

1 pound large shrimp, peeled and deveined (tail on or off based on preference)

2 tablespoons olive oil

3 cloves garlic, minced

2 tablespoons fresh parsley, finely chopped

1 teaspoon lemon zest

Salt and pepper to taste

Lemon wedges for serving

NUTRITIONAL INFORMATION (per serving):

Calories: 180 • **Total Fat:** 8g • **Saturated Fat:** 1g • **Cholesterol:** 220mg • **Sodium:** 880mg • **Total Carbohydrates:** 2g • **Dietary Fiber:** 0g • **Sugars:** 0g • **Protein:** 24g

DIRECTIONS:

1. **Prepare the Shrimp:** In a large bowl, combine the shrimp with olive oil, minced garlic, chopped parsley, lemon zest, salt, and pepper. Toss until the shrimp are evenly coated with the seasoning.

2. **Marinate:** Let the shrimp marinate for about 10 minutes at room temperature to enhance the flavors.

3. Preheat the air fryer to 400°F (200°C).

4. **Air Fry the Shrimp:**

   a. Arrange the shrimp in a single layer in the air fryer basket. Depending on the size of your air fryer, you may need to cook the shrimp in batches to avoid overcrowding.

   b. Air fry for 6-8 minutes or until the shrimp are pink, firm, and cooked through. There's no need to turn them halfway through cooking if they are in a single layer.

5. **Serve:** Transfer the cooked shrimp to a serving platter. Serve immediately with lemon wedges on the side for squeezing over the shrimp.

Mediterranean Air-Fried Calamari Rings

Yield: *4 servings* | Prep Time: *20 minutes (includes marinating time)* | Cook Time: *8 minutes*

INGREDIENTS:

1 pound calamari, cleaned and cut into 1/2-inch rings

1/2 cup buttermilk

1 cup all-purpose flour

1 teaspoon paprika

1 teaspoon garlic powder

1 teaspoon dried oregano

Salt and pepper to taste

Lemon wedges for serving

Optional: Fresh parsley, chopped for garnish

Optional: Marinara sauce or aioli for dipping

NUTRITIONAL INFORMATION (per serving):

Calories: 230 • **Total Fat:** 2g • **Saturated Fat:** 0.5g • **Cholesterol:** 264mg • **Sodium:** 175mg • **Total Carbohydrates:** 27g • **Dietary Fiber:** 1g • **Sugars:** 2g • **Protein:** 24g

DIRECTIONS:

1. **Marinate the Calamari:** In a bowl, soak the calamari rings in buttermilk for at least 15 minutes. This process helps tenderize the calamari and adds flavor.

2. **Prepare the Coating:** In another bowl, mix together the all-purpose flour, paprika, garlic powder, dried oregano, salt, and pepper.

3. **Coat the Calamari:** Remove the calamari from the buttermilk, letting excess drip off. Dredge the calamari rings in the flour mixture until well coated. Shake off any excess flour.

4. Preheat the air fryer to 400°F (200°C).

5. **Air Fry the Calamari:**

   a. Place the coated calamari rings in the air fryer basket in a single layer, making sure they do not touch. You may need to cook in batches depending on the size of your air fryer.

   b. Air fry for 8 minutes, or until the calamari is golden brown and crispy, shaking the basket halfway through cooking.

6. Serve the air-fried calamari rings immediately with lemon wedges on the side. Garnish with chopped parsley if desired. Also can be served alongside marinara sauce or aioli for dipping, if preferred

Air-Fried Octopus with Olive Oil and Paprika

Yield: *4 servings* | Prep Time: *15 minutes (plus boiling time)* | Cook Time: *10 minutes*

INGREDIENTS:

1 large octopus tentacle (about 1 pound), pre-boiled until tender

2 tablespoons olive oil

1 teaspoon smoked paprika

1/2 teaspoon garlic powder

Salt and freshly ground black pepper to taste

Lemon wedges for serving

Fresh parsley, chopped for garnish

NUTRITIONAL INFORMATION (per serving):

Calories: 180 • **Total Fat:** 7g • **Saturated Fat:** 1g • **Cholesterol:** 75mg • **Sodium:** 300mg • **Total Carbohydrates:** 2g • **Dietary Fiber:** 0g • **Sugars:** 0g • **Protein:** 25g

DIRECTIONS:

1. **Prep the Octopus:** If not already pre-boiled, clean the octopus tentacle and boil in salted water for about 60-90 minutes, or until tender. Allow it to cool, then cut into bite-sized pieces.

2. **Season the Octopus:** In a bowl, toss the boiled octopus pieces with olive oil, smoked paprika, garlic powder, salt, and pepper until well coated.

3. Preheat the air fryer to 400°F (200°C).

4. **Air Fry the Octopus:**

   a. Arrange the seasoned octopus pieces in the air fryer basket in a single layer. Depending on the size of your air fryer, you may need to cook in batches.

   b. Air fry for 10 minutes, or until the octopus is crispy on the outside and tender on the inside.

5. Serve the air-fried octopus immediately, garnished with chopped fresh parsley and accompanied by lemon wedges on the side.

Garlic Lemon Air-Fried Prawns

Yield: *4 servings* | Prep Time: *10 minutes (plus marinating time)* | Cook Time: *8 minutes*

INGREDIENTS:

1 pound large prawns, peeled and deveined (tails left on)

3 tablespoons olive oil

4 cloves garlic, minced

Juice and zest of 1 lemon

1 teaspoon red pepper flakes (adjust to taste)

Salt and freshly ground black pepper to taste

Fresh parsley, chopped for garnish

Lemon wedges for serving

NUTRITIONAL INFORMATION (per serving):

Calories: 200 • **Total Fat:** 10g • **Saturated Fat:** 1.5g • **Cholesterol:** 180mg • **Sodium:** 300mg • **Total Carbohydrates:** 3g • **Dietary Fiber:** 0g • **Sugars:** 0g • **Protein:** 24g

DIRECTIONS:

1. **Marinate the Prawns:**

   a. In a large bowl, combine olive oil, minced garlic, lemon juice, lemon zest, red pepper flakes, salt, and black pepper. Whisk to blend.

   b. Add the prawns to the marinade and toss to coat evenly. Cover and refrigerate for at least 30 minutes to allow the flavors to meld.

2. Preheat the air fryer to 400°F (200°C).

3. **Air Fry the Prawns:**

   a. Remove the prawns from the marinade, letting excess drip off. Arrange the prawns in the air fryer basket in a single layer, ensuring they are not overcrowded. You may need to cook in batches depending on the size of your air fryer.

   b. Air fry for 6-8 minutes or until the prawns are pink, opaque, and cooked through.

4. **Serve:** Transfer the cooked prawns to a serving platter. Garnish with chopped fresh parsley and serve with lemon wedges on the side.

Air-Fried Crab Cakes with Aioli

Yield: *4 servings (8 crab cakes)* │ Prep Time: *20 minutes* │ Cook Time: *10 minutes*

INGREDIENTS:

For Crab Cakes:

1 pound lump crab meat, picked over for shells

1 cup breadcrumbs, divided

1/4 cup mayonnaise

1 large egg, beaten

2 tablespoons fresh parsley, finely chopped

1 teaspoon Dijon mustard

1 teaspoon Worcestershire sauce

1/2 teaspoon paprika

Salt and pepper to taste

Lemon wedges for serving

For Aioli:

1/2 cup mayonnaise

1 clove garlic, minced

1 tablespoon lemon juice

1/2 teaspoon paprika

Salt and pepper to taste

NUTRITIONAL INFORMATION
(per serving, 2 crab cakes with aioli):

Calories: 380 • Total Fat: 24g • Saturated Fat: 4g • Cholesterol: 125mg • Sodium: 800mg • Total Carbohydrates: 19g • Dietary Fiber: 1g • Sugars: 2g • Protein: 24g

DIRECTIONS:

1. **Prepare the Crab Cakes:**

   a. In a large bowl, gently mix together the crab meat, 1/2 cup breadcrumbs, mayonnaise, beaten egg, parsley, Dijon mustard, Worcestershire sauce, paprika, salt, and pepper until well combined.

   b. Shape the mixture into 8 equal-sized cakes. Coat each crab cake lightly with the remaining breadcrumbs. Chill in the refrigerator for at least 10 minutes to firm up.

2. **Make the Aioli:** In a small bowl, whisk together mayonnaise, minced garlic, lemon juice, paprika, salt, and pepper. Adjust seasoning to taste. Refrigerate until ready to serve.

3. Preheat the air fryer to 400°F (200°C).

4. **Air Fry the Crab Cakes:**

   a. Spray the air fryer basket with non-stick cooking spray. Place the crab cakes in the basket, making sure they are not touching. Work in batches if necessary.

   b. Air fry for 10 minutes, flipping halfway through, or until the crab cakes are golden brown and heated through.

5. Serve the air-fried crab cakes hot with the prepared aioli and lemon wedges on the side.

Air-Fried Sea Bass with Mediterranean Salsa

Yield: *4 servings* │ Prep Time: *15 minutes* │ Cook Time: *12 minutes*

INGREDIENTS:

For Sea Bass:

4 sea bass fillets (about 6 ounces each)

2 tablespoons olive oil

1 teaspoon lemon zest

Salt and pepper to taste

For Mediterranean Salsa:

1 cup cherry tomatoes, quartered

1/2 cup cucumber, diced

1/4 cup red onion, finely chopped

1/4 cup Kalamata olives, pitted and sliced

1/4 cup feta cheese, crumbled

2 tablespoons fresh parsley, chopped

2 tablespoons fresh lemon juice

1 tablespoon olive oil

Salt and pepper to taste

DIRECTIONS:

1. **Prepare the Sea Bass:** Rinse the sea bass fillets and pat dry with paper towels. Mix 2 tablespoons olive oil with lemon zest, salt, and pepper. Brush this mixture over both sides of the sea bass fillets.

2. Preheat the air fryer to 400°F (200°C).

3. **Air Fry the Sea Bass:**

   a. Place the sea bass fillets in the air fryer basket, ensuring they do not overlap. You may need to cook in batches depending on the size of your air fryer.

   b. Air fry for 10-12 minutes or until the fish flakes easily with a fork.

4. **Prepare the Mediterranean Salsa:** While the fish is cooking, in a bowl, combine cherry tomatoes, cucumber, red onion, Kalamata olives, feta cheese, parsley, lemon juice, and 1 tablespoon olive oil. Season with salt and pepper to taste and toss gently to mix.

5. **Serve:** Once the sea bass is cooked, transfer the fillets to serving plates. Top each fillet with a generous portion of the Mediterranean salsa. Optionally, garnish with additional parsley or lemon wedges before serving.

NUTRITIONAL INFORMATION
(per serving):

Calories: 320 • **Total Fat:** 18g • **Saturated Fat:** 4g • **Cholesterol:** 85mg • **Sodium:** 300mg • **Total Carbohydrates:** 6g • **Dietary Fiber:** 1g • **Sugars:** 2g • **Protein:** 34g

Air-Fried Clams with a Breadcrumb Topping

Yield: *4 servings* | Prep Time: *15 minutes* | Cook Time: *6 minutes*

INGREDIENTS:

24 littleneck clams, scrubbed clean

1/2 cup breadcrumbs

2 tablespoons grated Parmesan cheese

2 cloves garlic, minced

2 tablespoons fresh parsley, finely chopped

Zest of 1 lemon

2 tablespoons olive oil

Salt and pepper to taste

Lemon wedges for serving

DIRECTIONS:

1. **Pre-cook the Clams:**

   a. In a large skillet over medium heat, add about 1/4 cup water and the clams. Cover and cook for 3-4 minutes or until the clams just start to open. Discard any clams that do not open.

   b. Remove the clams from the skillet and let them cool slightly. Detach the clam meat from one shell half, discarding the other half, so each clam sits in its half shell.

2. **Prepare the Breadcrumb Topping:** In a bowl, combine breadcrumbs, grated Parmesan, minced garlic, chopped parsley, lemon zest, olive oil, salt, and pepper. Mix until well combined.

3. Preheat the air fryer to 400°F (200°C).

4. **Top the Clams:** Spoon the breadcrumb mixture on top of each clam, pressing gently to adhere.

5. **Air Fry the Clams:**

   a. Arrange the clams in the air fryer basket, breadcrumb side up. Depending on the size of your air fryer, you may need to cook in batches.

   b. Air fry for 6 minutes or until the breadcrumb topping is golden and crispy.

6. **Serve:** Carefully remove the clams from the air fryer and place them on a serving platter. Serve immediately with lemon wedges on the side.

NUTRITIONAL INFORMATION
(per serving):

Calories: 190 • **Total Fat:** 9g • **Saturated Fat:** 2g • **Cholesterol:** 20mg • **Sodium:** 300mg • **Total Carbohydrates:** 14g • **Dietary Fiber:** 1g • **Sugars:** 1g • **Protein:** 12g

Spicy Air-Fried Mussels with Tomato Sauce

Yield: *4 servings* | Prep Time: *15 minutes* | Cook Time: *8 minutes*

INGREDIENTS:

For Mussels:

2 pounds mussels, cleaned and debearded

1 tablespoon olive oil

1/2 teaspoon red pepper flakes (adjust to taste)

Salt to taste

For Spicy Tomato Sauce:

2 tablespoons olive oil

3 cloves garlic, minced

1 small onion, finely chopped

1 can (14 oz) crushed tomatoes

1 teaspoon dried oregano

1/2 teaspoon red pepper flakes (adjust for desired spiciness)

Salt and pepper to taste

Fresh basil leaves, chopped for garnish

NUTRITIONAL INFORMATION (per serving):

Calories: 280 • Total Fat: 15g • Saturated Fat: 2g • Cholesterol: 50mg • Sodium: 700mg • Total Carbohydrates: 15g • Dietary Fiber: 2g • Sugars: 6g • Protein: 22g

DIRECTIONS:

1. **Prepare the Spicy Tomato Sauce:**

   a. Heat 2 tablespoons of olive oil in a saucepan over medium heat. Add the minced garlic and chopped onion, sautéing until the onion is translucent and the garlic is fragrant, about 3 minutes.

   b. Stir in the crushed tomatoes, dried oregano, red pepper flakes, salt, and pepper. Bring to a simmer and cook for about 10 minutes, until the sauce thickens slightly. Adjust seasoning as needed.

   c. Keep the sauce warm while you air fry the mussels.

2. Preheat the air fryer to 400°F (200°C).

3. **Prepare the Mussels:** In a large bowl, toss the cleaned mussels with 1 tablespoon olive oil, red pepper flakes, and a pinch of salt until well coated.

4. **Air Fry the Mussels:**

   a. Arrange the mussels in the air fryer basket, ensuring they are in a single layer. Depending on the size of your air fryer, you may need to cook in batches.

   b. Air fry for 6-8 minutes or until the mussels have opened and are cooked through. Discard any mussels that do not open.

5. **Serve:**

   a. Spoon a generous amount of the spicy tomato sauce onto serving plates or a platter.

   b. Arrange the air-fried mussels on top of the sauce.

   c. Garnish with chopped fresh basil.

6. **Optional Serving Suggestion:** Serve with crusty bread to soak up the delicious sauce.

Air-Fried Swordfish with Olive Oil and Oregano

Yield: *2 servings* | Prep Time: *10 minutes* (plus marinating time) | Cook Time: *10 minutes*

INGREDIENTS:

2 swordfish steaks (about 6 ounces each)

2 tablespoons olive oil

1 tablespoon fresh lemon juice

2 cloves garlic, minced

1 teaspoon dried oregano

Salt and pepper to taste

Lemon slices and fresh oregano for garnish

DIRECTIONS:

1. **Marinate the Swordfish:**

   a. In a small bowl, whisk together olive oil, lemon juice, minced garlic, dried oregano, salt, and pepper.

   b. Place the swordfish steaks in a shallow dish or a resealable plastic bag. Pour the marinade over the steaks, making sure they are well coated.

   c. Refrigerate and let marinate for at least 30 minutes or up to 2 hours for more flavor.

2. Preheat the air fryer to 400°F (200°C).

3. **Prepare the Swordfish for Cooking:** Remove the swordfish steaks from the marinade, letting excess drip off. Discard the remaining marinade.

4. **Air Fry the Swordfish:**

   a. Place the marinated swordfish steaks in the air fryer basket. Make sure they are not touching to ensure even cooking.

   b. Air fry for 10 minutes, flipping halfway through, or until the fish is cooked through and easily flakes with a fork. The exact cooking time may vary based on the thickness of the steaks.

5. **Serve:**

   a. Carefully remove the swordfish steaks from the air fryer.

   b. Serve immediately, garnished with lemon slices and fresh oregano.

NUTRITIONAL INFORMATION
(per serving):

Calories: 280 • **Total Fat:** 15g • **Saturated Fat:** 3g • **Cholesterol:** 90mg • **Sodium:** 150mg • **Total Carbohydrates:** 1g • **Dietary Fiber:** 0g • **Sugars:** 0g • **Protein:** 34g

Lemon Garlic Air-Fried Haddock

Yield: *4 servings* | Prep Time: *10 minutes* | Cook Time: *12 minutes*

INGREDIENTS:

4 haddock fillets (about 6 ounces each)

2 tablespoons olive oil

2 cloves garlic, minced

Juice of 1 lemon, plus additional lemon wedges for serving

1 teaspoon lemon zest

1/2 teaspoon dried thyme

Salt and pepper to taste

Fresh parsley, chopped for garnish

DIRECTIONS:

1. **Prepare the Lemon Garlic Marinade:** In a small bowl, combine olive oil, minced garlic, lemon juice, lemon zest, dried thyme, salt, and pepper. Whisk together until well mixed.

2. **Marinate the Haddock:**

   a. Place the haddock fillets in a shallow dish or a resealable plastic bag. Pour the lemon garlic marinade over the fillets, making sure each piece is well coated.

   b. Let the fillets marinate in the refrigerator for 15-30 minutes.

3. Preheat the air fryer to 400°F (200°C).

4. **Air Fry the Haddock:**

   a. Remove the haddock fillets from the marinade and let the excess drip off. Discard the remaining marinade.

   b. Place the fillets in the air fryer basket in a single layer, ensuring they do not overlap. You may need to cook in batches depending on the size of your air fryer.

   c. Air fry for 10-12 minutes, or until the haddock is cooked through and flakes easily with a fork.

5. **Serve:**

   a. Carefully remove the haddock fillets from the air fryer and transfer them to serving plates.

   b. Garnish with fresh parsley and serve with lemon wedges on the side.

NUTRITIONAL INFORMATION
(per serving):

Calories: 200 • **Total Fat:** 7g • **Saturated Fat:** 1g • **Cholesterol:** 90mg • **Sodium:** 125mg • **Total Carbohydrates:** 1g • **Dietary Fiber:** 0g • **Sugars:** 0g • **Protein:** 34g

Chapter 7

Poultry and Meat

Italian Pesto Chicken Thighs

Yield: *4 servings* | Prep Time: *10 minutes* | Cook Time: *20 minutes*

INGREDIENTS:

8 boneless, skinless chicken thighs

Salt and pepper to taste

1/2 cup basil pesto (store-bought or homemade)

2 tablespoons olive oil

1 tablespoon lemon juice

1 clove garlic, minced

Optional: Grated Parmesan cheese for garnish

Optional: Fresh basil leaves for garnish

NUTRITIONAL INFORMATION (per serving):

Calories: 400 • **Total Fat:** 28g • **Saturated Fat:** 6g • **Cholesterol:** 180mg • **Sodium:** 400mg • **Total Carbohydrates:** 2g • **Dietary Fiber:** 0g • **Sugars:** 1g • **Protein:** 35g

DIRECTIONS:

1. **Prep the Chicken:** Season the chicken thighs with salt and pepper on both sides.

2. **Marinate:** In a large bowl, mix together the basil pesto, olive oil, lemon juice, and minced garlic. Add the chicken thighs and toss until they are well coated with the pesto mixture. Let marinate for at least 30 minutes in the refrigerator, if time allows.

3. Preheat the air fryer to 380°F (190°C).

4. **Air Fry the Chicken:**

   a. Arrange the chicken thighs in the air fryer basket in a single layer. Depending on the size of your air fryer, you may need to cook in batches.

   b. Air fry for 18-20 minutes, or until the chicken is cooked through and the internal temperature reaches 165°F (74°C).

5. **Serve:** Transfer the cooked chicken thighs to a serving platter. Optionally, sprinkle with grated Parmesan cheese and garnish with fresh basil leaves before serving.

Air-Fried Chicken with Artichokes and Olives

Yield: *4 servings* | Prep Time: *15 minutes* | Cook Time: *25 minutes*

INGREDIENTS:

4 boneless, skinless chicken breasts

Salt and pepper to taste

1 tablespoon olive oil

1 teaspoon dried oregano

1 teaspoon dried thyme

1 cup artichoke hearts, quartered (canned or jarred, drained)

1/2 cup Kalamata olives, pitted

2 cloves garlic, minced

1 lemon, sliced into rounds

Optional: Fresh parsley, chopped for garnish

NUTRITIONAL INFORMATION (per serving):

Calories: 280 • **Total Fat:** 12g • **Saturated Fat:** 2g • **Cholesterol:** 95mg • **Sodium:** 480mg • **Total Carbohydrates:** 8g • **Dietary Fiber:** 3g • **Sugars:** 2g • **Protein:** 36g

DIRECTIONS:

1. Season both sides of the chicken breasts with salt and pepper. Drizzle olive oil over the chicken and sprinkle with oregano and thyme, ensuring they're well coated.

2. Preheat the air fryer to 375°F (190°C).

3. **Prepare the Chicken for Air Frying:**

   a. In a bowl, mix together the artichoke hearts, Kalamata olives, and minced garlic. Set aside.

   b. Place the seasoned chicken breasts in the air fryer basket. Arrange lemon slices over the chicken. Scatter the artichoke and olive mixture around the chicken in the basket.

4. **Air Fry the Chicken:** Air fry for 22-25 minutes, or until the chicken is cooked through and reaches an internal temperature of 165°F (74°C). If your air fryer model requires, flip the chicken halfway through cooking and stir the artichoke and olive mixture.

5. **Serve:** Once cooked, remove the chicken breasts and place them on serving plates. Spoon the artichoke and olive mixture around the chicken. Garnish with fresh parsley if desired.

6. **Optional Serving Suggestion:** Serve alongside a simple Mediterranean salad or overcooked quinoa for a complete meal.

Moroccan Spiced Chicken Drumsticks

Yield: *4 servings* | Prep Time: *15 minutes (plus marinating time)* | Cook Time: *20 minutes*

INGREDIENTS:

8 chicken drumsticks, skin on
2 tablespoons olive oil
1 tablespoon ground cumin
1 tablespoon paprika
1 teaspoon ground cinnamon
1 teaspoon ground ginger
1/2 teaspoon ground turmeric
1/2 teaspoon cayenne pepper (adjust to taste)
2 cloves garlic, minced
Juice of 1 lemon
Salt and pepper to taste
Fresh cilantro, chopped for garnish

NUTRITIONAL INFORMATION
(per serving):

Calories: 320 • **Total Fat:** 18g • **Saturated Fat:** 4g • **Cholesterol:** 145mg • **Sodium:** 200mg • **Total Carbohydrates:** 3g • **Dietary Fiber:** 1g • **Sugars:** 0g • **Protein:** 36g

DIRECTIONS:

1. **Marinate the Chicken:** In a large bowl, whisk together olive oil, cumin, paprika, cinnamon, ginger, turmeric, cayenne pepper, minced garlic, lemon juice, salt, and pepper. Add the chicken drumsticks and toss until they are well coated with the marinade. Cover and refrigerate for at least 2 hours or overnight for the best flavor.

2. Preheat the air fryer to 380°F (190°C).

3. **Air Fry the Chicken:**

   a. Arrange the marinated chicken drumsticks in the air fryer basket, making sure they are not touching. You may need to cook in batches depending on the size of your air fryer.

   b. Air fry for 20 minutes, turning the drumsticks halfway through, until the chicken is cooked through and the skin is crispy.

4. **Serve:** Transfer the cooked chicken drumsticks to a serving platter. Garnish with chopped fresh cilantro. Serve hot, accompanied by couscous, rice, or a fresh salad.

Turkish Sumac Chicken Kebabs

Yield: *4 servings* · Prep Time: *20 minutes (plus marinating time)* · Cook Time: *15 minutes*

INGREDIENTS:

2 pounds chicken breast, cut into 1-inch cubes
2 tablespoons olive oil
3 tablespoons sumac
2 cloves garlic, minced
Juice of 1 lemon
1 teaspoon paprika
1/2 teaspoon ground cumin
Salt and pepper to taste
1 red onion, cut into chunks
1 bell pepper, cut into chunks
Wooden or metal skewers (if using wooden skewers, soak in water for at least 30 minutes before use)

NUTRITIONAL INFORMATION
(per serving):

Calories: 310 • **Total Fat:** 10g • **Saturated Fat:** 1.5g • **Cholesterol:** 145mg • **Sodium:** 200mg • **Total Carbohydrates:** 6g • **Dietary Fiber:** 2g • **Sugars:** 2g • **Protein:** 48g

DIRECTIONS:

1. **Marinate the Chicken:** In a large bowl, mix together olive oil, sumac, minced garlic, lemon juice, paprika, cumin, salt, and pepper. Add the chicken cubes to the bowl and toss until they are well coated with the marinade. Cover and let marinate in the refrigerator for at least 1 hour, preferably longer.

2. Preheat the air fryer to 400°F (200°C).

3. **Assemble the Kebabs:** Thread the marinated chicken cubes onto skewers, alternating with chunks of red onion and bell pepper.

4. **Air Fry the Kebabs:**

   a. Place the skewers in the air fryer basket, ensuring they do not touch each other. Depending on the size of your air fryer, you may need to cook the kebabs in batches.

   b. Air fry for 12-15 minutes, turning the skewers halfway through, until the chicken is cooked through and slightly charred on the edges.

5. Serve the kebabs hot, garnished with fresh herbs if desired. They pair well with rice, flatbread, or a simple salad.

Lemon and Herb Air Fryer Turkey Cutlets

Yield: **4 servings** | Prep Time: **10 minutes (plus 30 minutes marinating time)** | Cook Time: **12 minutes**

INGREDIENTS:

4 turkey breast cutlets (about 1 pound)

2 tablespoons olive oil

Zest of 1 lemon

2 tablespoons fresh lemon juice

2 garlic cloves, minced

1 tablespoon fresh rosemary, chopped

1 tablespoon fresh thyme, chopped

1 tablespoon fresh parsley, chopped

Salt and freshly ground black pepper, to taste

Lemon slices, for garnish

NUTRITIONAL INFORMATION
(per serving):

Calories: 180 • Protein: 24g • Fat: 9g
(Saturated: 1.5g, Unsaturated: 7.5g) •
Carbohydrates: 2g • Fiber: 0.5g • Sugar: 0.5g
• Sodium: 75mg

DIRECTIONS:

1. **Marinate the Cutlets:** In a small bowl, whisk together olive oil, lemon zest, lemon juice, minced garlic, rosemary, thyme, parsley, salt, and pepper. Place the turkey cutlets in a shallow dish or a resealable plastic bag. Pour the marinade over the cutlets, ensuring they are well-coated. Cover or seal and refrigerate for at least 30 minutes to allow the flavors to infuse.

2. Preheat the air fryer to 380°F (193°C) for about 5 minutes.

3. **Prepare for Cooking:** Remove the turkey cutlets from the marinade, letting the excess drip off. Discard the remaining marinade.

4. **Cook the Cutlets:** Place the turkey cutlets in the air fryer basket in a single layer. You may need to cook them in batches to avoid overcrowding. Air fry for 6 minutes, then flip the cutlets and continue cooking for another 6 minutes, or until the cutlets are golden and reach an internal temperature of 165°F (74°C).

5. **Serve:** Transfer the cooked turkey cutlets to a serving plate. Garnish with lemon slices and a sprinkle of fresh parsley. Serve immediately.

Spicy Mediterranean Turkey Burgers

Yield: Serves 4 | Prep Time: **15 minutes** | Cook Time: **10 minutes**

INGREDIENTS:

Ingredients:

1 pound ground turkey (preferably lean)

1/4 cup red onion, finely chopped

1/4 cup fresh parsley, finely chopped

2 tablespoons sun-dried tomatoes, chopped

2 garlic cloves, minced

1 teaspoon cumin

1 teaspoon smoked paprika

1/2 teaspoon red pepper flakes (adjust for spice level)

Salt and freshly ground black pepper, to taste

4 whole wheat burger buns

Optional toppings: lettuce, tomato slices, cucumber, tzatziki sauce

NUTRITIONAL INFORMATION
(per serving, excluding toppings):

Calories: 260 • Protein: 27g • Fat: 6g
(Saturated: 1.5g, Unsaturated: 4.5g) •
Carbohydrates: 23g • Fiber: 3g • Sugar: 4g •
Sodium: 320mg

DIRECTIONS:

1. **Prepare the Burger Mixture:** In a large bowl, combine the ground turkey, red onion, parsley, sun-dried tomatoes, minced garlic, cumin, smoked paprika, red pepper flakes, salt, and pepper. Mix until just combined, being careful not to overmix to keep the burgers tender.

2. **Form the Patties:** Divide the mixture into 4 equal portions and form each into a burger patty. Make a small indentation in the center of each patty to prevent bulging during cooking.

3. Preheat the air fryer to 360°F (182°C) for about 3 minutes.

4. **Cook the Burgers:** Place the patties in the air fryer basket, ensuring they are not touching. Cook for 10 minutes, flipping halfway through, or until the burgers are cooked through and reach an internal temperature of 165°F (74°C).

5. **Prepare the Buns:** If desired, toast the whole wheat burger buns in the air fryer at 360°F (182°C) for 1-2 minutes, or until lightly toasted.

6. **Assemble the Burgers:** Place each turkey patty on a bun and add your preferred toppings, such as lettuce, tomato slices, cucumber, and a dollop of tzatziki sauce.

Greek-Style Air Fryer Turkey Meatballs

Yield: Serves 4 | Prep Time: *15 minutes* | Cook Time: *10 minutes*

INGREDIENTS:

1 pound ground turkey

1/4 cup breadcrumbs

1 large egg

1/4 cup feta cheese, crumbled

1/4 cup red onion, finely chopped

2 tablespoons fresh parsley, chopped

2 garlic cloves, minced

1 teaspoon dried oregano

Zest of 1 lemon

Salt and freshly ground black pepper, to taste

Olive oil spray (for coating)

NUTRITIONAL INFORMATION (per serving):

Calories: 220 • Protein: 27g • Fat: 10g (Saturated: 3g, Unsaturated: 7g) • Carbohydrates: 7g • Fiber: 0.5g • Sugar: 1g • Sodium: 320mg

DIRECTIONS:

1. **Mix the Ingredients:** In a large bowl, combine ground turkey, breadcrumbs, egg, feta cheese, red onion, parsley, garlic, oregano, lemon zest, salt, and pepper. Mix until just combined, being careful not to overwork the mixture to keep the meatballs tender.

2. **Form the Meatballs:** With moistened hands, form the mixture into 16 meatballs, about the size of a golf ball.

3. **Preheat the Air Fryer:** Preheat the air fryer to 400°F (200°C) for about 3 minutes.

4. **Prepare for Cooking:** Lightly spray the air fryer basket with olive oil spray. Arrange the meatballs in the basket, making sure they are not touching. You may need to cook them in batches, depending on the size of your air fryer.

5. **Cook the Meatballs:** Air fry for 10 minutes or until the meatballs are browned on the outside and cooked through, reaching an internal temperature of 165°F (74°C). Shake the basket halfway through cooking to ensure even browning.

6. Serve the meatballs hot, garnished with additional chopped parsley and lemon wedges on the side.

Greek-Style Air-Fried Lamb Chops

Yield: *4 servings* | Prep Time: *15 minutes (plus marinating time)* | Cook Time: *10 minutes*

INGREDIENTS:

8 lamb chops (about 1-inch thick)

1/4 cup olive oil

Juice of 1 lemon

4 cloves garlic, minced

2 tablespoons fresh oregano, chopped (or 2 teaspoons dried oregano)

1 teaspoon dried thyme

1 teaspoon rosemary, chopped (or 1/2 teaspoon dried rosemary)

Salt and pepper to taste

Lemon wedges and fresh parsley for garnish

NUTRITIONAL INFORMATION (per serving):

Calories: 410 • Total Fat: 30g • Saturated Fat: 11g • Cholesterol: 120mg • Sodium: 200mg • Total Carbohydrates: 2g • Dietary Fiber: 0g • Sugars: 0g • Protein: 32g

DIRECTIONS:

1. **Prepare the Marinade:** In a large bowl, whisk together olive oil, lemon juice, minced garlic, oregano, thyme, rosemary, salt, and pepper.

2. **Marinate the Lamb:** Add the lamb chops to the marinade, ensuring they are well coated on all sides. Cover the bowl and refrigerate for at least 2 hours or overnight for the best flavor.

3. Preheat the air fryer to 400°F (200°C).

4. **Air Fry the Lamb Chops:**

   a. Remove the lamb chops from the marinade, letting the excess drip off. Arrange the chops in the air fryer basket in a single layer. You may need to work in batches depending on the size of your air fryer.

   b. Air fry for 10 minutes for medium-rare (adjust the time if you prefer your lamb more or less done), flipping halfway through the cooking time.

5. **Serve:** Let the lamb chops rest for a few minutes after cooking. Serve garnished with lemon wedges and fresh parsley.

Crispy Air-Fried Chicken Souvlaki

Yield: *4 servings* | Prep Time: *15 minutes* (plus marinating time) | Cook Time: *15 minutes*

INGREDIENTS:

For Chicken Souvlaki:

1.5 pounds chicken breast, cut into 1-inch cubes

3 tablespoons olive oil

Juice of 1 lemon

2 cloves garlic, minced

1 tablespoon dried oregano

1 teaspoon paprika

Salt and pepper to taste

For Serving:

Pita bread or flatbreads, warmed

Tzatziki sauce (store-bought or homemade)

Chopped tomatoes

Sliced red onions

Chopped cucumbers

Fresh parsley, for garnish

NUTRITIONAL INFORMATION
(per serving, chicken only):

Calories: 280 • **Total Fat:** 12g • **Saturated Fat:** 2g • **Cholesterol:** 110mg • **Sodium:** 200mg • **Total Carbohydrates:** 3g • **Dietary Fiber:** 1g • **Sugars:** 1g • **Protein:** 38g

DIRECTIONS:

1. **Marinate the Chicken:** In a large bowl, whisk together olive oil, lemon juice, minced garlic, dried oregano, paprika, salt, and pepper. Add the chicken cubes to the marinade, ensuring they are fully coated. Cover and refrigerate for at least 2 hours or overnight for best results.

2. Preheat the air fryer to 400°F (200°C).

3. **Air Fry the Chicken:**

   a. Thread the marinated chicken cubes onto skewers (if using wooden skewers, soak them in water for at least 30 minutes beforehand to prevent burning).

   b. Place the chicken skewers in the air fryer basket, leaving some space between each skewer for even cooking. You may need to cook in batches depending on the size of your air fryer.

   c. Air fry for 12-15 minutes, turning halfway through or until the chicken is fully cooked and has a nice golden color.

4. Serve the chicken souvlaki on warmed pita bread or flatbreads, topped with tzatziki sauce, chopped tomatoes, sliced red onions, and chopped cucumbers. Garnish with fresh parsley.

Moroccan Air-Fried Meatballs (Kefta)

Yield: *4 servings* | Prep Time: *20 minutes* | Cook Time: *10 minutes*

INGREDIENTS:

1 pound ground lamb or beef (or a mix of both)

1 small onion, finely grated

2 cloves garlic, minced

1/4 cup fresh parsley, finely chopped

1/4 cup fresh cilantro, finely chopped

1 teaspoon ground cumin

1 teaspoon smoked paprika

1/2 teaspoon ground cinnamon

1/4 teaspoon cayenne pepper (adjust to taste)

Salt and pepper to taste

1 egg

1/2 cup breadcrumbs

For Serving:

Yogurt or tahini sauce (optional)

Fresh mint or additional parsley for garnish

NUTRITIONAL INFORMATION
(per serving):

Calories: 350 • **Total Fat:** 20g • **Saturated Fat:** 8g • **Cholesterol:** 120mg • **Sodium:** 300mg • **Total Carbohydrates:** 12g • **Dietary Fiber:** 1g • **Sugars:** 2g • **Protein:** 28g

DIRECTIONS:

1. **Mix the Meatball Ingredients:** In a large bowl, combine the ground meat, grated onion, minced garlic, chopped parsley, chopped cilantro, cumin, paprika, cinnamon, cayenne pepper, salt, pepper, egg, and breadcrumbs. Mix until just combined, being careful not to overwork the mixture.

2. **Form the Meatballs:** Shape the mixture into small meatballs, about 1 inch in diameter. You should have around 20 to 24 meatballs.

3. Preheat the air fryer to 400°F (200°C).

4. **Air Fry the Meatballs:**

   a. Arrange the meatballs in the air fryer basket, ensuring they are not touching. Depending on the size of your air fryer, you may need to cook in batches.

   b. Air fry for 10 minutes, or until the meatballs are browned and cooked through, shaking the basket halfway through the cooking time.

5. Serve the Moroccan meatballs hot, garnished with fresh mint or parsley. Offer yogurt or tahini sauce on the side for dipping, if desired.

Air-Fried Prosciutto-Wrapped Pork Tenderloin

Yield: *4 servings* | Prep Time: *15 minutes* | Cook Time: *20 minutes*

INGREDIENTS:

1 pork tenderloin (about 1 to 1.5 pounds)

Salt and pepper to taste

1 tablespoon fresh rosemary, chopped

1 tablespoon olive oil

8 slices of prosciutto

2 cloves garlic, minced

DIRECTIONS:

1. **Prep the Pork Tenderloin:** Trim any excess fat from the pork tenderloin. Season all sides with salt, pepper, and chopped rosemary.

2. **Wrap with Prosciutto:** Lay out the slices of prosciutto on a flat surface, slightly overlapping. Place the seasoned pork tenderloin at one end and roll it up tightly in the prosciutto, ensuring it is completely covered.

3. Preheat the air fryer to 390°F (200°C).

4. **Air Fry the Pork:**

    a. Rub the outside of the prosciutto-wrapped pork tenderloin with olive oil and sprinkle minced garlic over it. Place the pork tenderloin in the air fryer basket.

    b. Air fry for 20 minutes or until the internal temperature of the pork reaches 145°F (63°C) when checked with a meat thermometer. For a well-done tenderloin, extend the cooking time as needed.

5. **Rest Before Serving:** Once cooked, let the pork tenderloin rest for 5 minutes before slicing. This allows the juices to redistribute throughout the meat, ensuring it is moist and tender.

6. **Serve:** Slice the pork tenderloin into medallions and serve immediately.

NUTRITIONAL INFORMATION (per serving):

Calories: 240 • **Total Fat:** 9g • **Saturated Fat:** 3g • **Cholesterol:** 90mg • **Sodium:** 720mg • **Total Carbohydrates:** 1g • **Dietary Fiber:** 0g • **Sugars:** 0g • **Protein:** 36g

Spanish Chorizo and Potato Hash

Yield: *4 servings* | Prep Time: *15 minutes* | Cook Time: *20 minutes*

INGREDIENTS:

1 pound potatoes, diced into 1/2-inch pieces

8 ounces Spanish chorizo, diced

1 large onion, diced

1 red bell pepper, diced

2 cloves garlic, minced

1 teaspoon smoked paprika

1/2 teaspoon cayenne pepper (adjust to taste)

Salt and pepper to taste

2 tablespoons olive oil

Optional: 4 eggs (for topping)

Optional: Fresh parsley, chopped for garnish

DIRECTIONS:

1. **Prep the Ingredients:** Wash and dice the potatoes, chorizo, onion, and red bell pepper. Mince the garlic.

2. **Season the Mixture:** In a large bowl, combine the diced potatoes, chorizo, onion, red bell pepper, minced garlic, smoked paprika, cayenne pepper, salt, pepper, and olive oil. Toss until everything is well coated with the seasoning and oil.

3. Preheat the air fryer to 400°F (200°C).

4. **Cook the Hash:**

    a. Transfer the chorizo and potato mixture to the air fryer basket, spreading it out into an even layer.

    b. Air fry for 15-20 minutes, shaking the basket halfway through the cooking time until the potatoes are crispy and golden brown.

5. **(Optional) Fry the Eggs:** While the hash is cooking, fry the eggs to your preferred doneness in a skillet over medium heat.

6. **Serve:** Divide the chorizo and potato hash among plates. If using, top each serving with a fried egg. Garnish with chopped fresh parsley before serving.

NUTRITIONAL INFORMATION (per serving, without egg):

Calories: 400 • **Total Fat:** 24g • **Saturated Fat:** 7g • **Cholesterol:** 45mg • **Sodium:** 800mg • **Total Carbohydrates:** 30g • **Dietary Fiber:** 4g • **Sugars:** 3g • **Protein:** 18g

Turkish Beef Patties with Sumac Onions

Yield: *4 servings* | Prep Time: *20 minutes* | Cook Time: *12 minutes*

INGREDIENTS:

For Beef Patties:

1 pound ground beef (preferably 85% lean)

1 small onion, finely grated

2 cloves garlic, minced

1/4 cup fresh parsley, finely chopped

1 teaspoon ground cumin

1 teaspoon paprika

1/2 teaspoon ground coriander

1/4 teaspoon cayenne pepper (adjust to taste)

Salt and pepper to taste

For Sumac Onions:

1 large red onion, thinly sliced

2 tablespoons sumac

1 tablespoon olive oil

1 tablespoon lemon juice

Salt to taste

NUTRITIONAL INFORMATION
(per serving):

Calories: 290 • **Total Fat:** 18g • **Saturated Fat:** 6g • **Cholesterol:** 80mg • **Sodium:** 200mg • **Total Carbohydrates:** 6g • **Dietary Fiber:** 1g • **Sugars:** 2g • **Protein:** 24g

DIRECTIONS:

1. **Prepare the Beef Mixture:** In a large bowl, combine the ground beef, grated onion, minced garlic, chopped parsley, cumin, paprika, coriander, cayenne pepper, salt, and pepper. Mix until well combined, but do not overmix.

2. **Form the Patties:** Divide the mixture into 8 equal parts and form each into a patty.

3. **Marinate the Onions:** In a separate bowl, combine the thinly sliced red onion, sumac, olive oil, lemon juice, and salt. Toss well and set aside to marinate while you cook the beef patties.

4. Preheat the air fryer to 400°F (200°C).

5. **Cook the Beef Patties:**

   a. Arrange the beef patties in the air fryer basket, making sure they do not touch. You may need to cook in batches depending on the size of your air fryer.

   b. Air fry for 10-12 minutes, flipping halfway through or until the patties are cooked through and have a nice crust.

6. Serve the beef patties hot, topped with the sumac onions. It can be served alongside pita bread, yogurt, or side salad for a complete meal.

Italian Sausage and Peppers

Yield: *4 servings* | Prep Time: *10 minutes* | Cook Time: *15 minutes*

INGREDIENTS:

4 Italian sausages (about 1 pound)

2 bell peppers (1 red, 1 green), sliced into strips

1 large onion, sliced into strips

2 tablespoons olive oil

1 teaspoon dried oregano

1/2 teaspoon garlic powder

Salt and pepper to taste

Optional: Crushed red pepper flakes for added heat

Optional: Fresh parsley, chopped for garnish

Optional: Hoagie rolls or Italian bread for serving

NUTRITIONAL INFORMATION
(per serving, without bread):

Calories: 400 • **Total Fat:** 29g • **Saturated Fat:** 10g • **Cholesterol:** 85mg • **Sodium:** 800mg • **Total Carbohydrates:** 10g • **Dietary Fiber:** 2g • **Sugars:** 4g • **Protein:** 22g

DIRECTIONS:

1. **Prep the Vegetables:** Toss the sliced bell peppers and onion with olive oil, dried oregano, garlic powder, salt, pepper, and crushed red pepper flakes (if using) until well coated.

2. Preheat the air fryer to 400°F (200°C).

3. **Cook Sausages and Vegetables:**

   a. Place the Italian sausages in the air fryer basket. Surround them with the seasoned bell peppers and onions, distributing them evenly.

   b. Air fry for 15 minutes, turning the sausages and stirring the vegetables halfway through until the sausages are cooked through and the vegetables are tender and slightly charred.

4. **Serve:** If desired, serve the sausages and peppers on hoagie rolls or with Italian bread on the side. Garnish with fresh parsley for a touch of color and freshness.

Lamb Kofta Kebabs with Yogurt Sauce

Yield: **4 servings** | Prep Time: **20 minutes** (plus **30 minutes for** chilling) | Cook Time: **10 minutes**

INGREDIENTS:

For Lamb Kofta Kebabs:

1 pound ground lamb

1 small onion, finely grated

2 cloves garlic, minced

2 tablespoons fresh parsley, finely chopped

2 tablespoons fresh mint, finely chopped

1 teaspoon ground cumin

1 teaspoon smoked paprika

1/2 teaspoon ground coriander

1/4 teaspoon ground cinnamon

Salt and pepper to taste

Wooden or metal skewers (if using wooden skewers, soak in water for at least 30 minutes before use)

For Yogurt Sauce:

1 cup Greek yogurt

1 clove garlic, minced

1 tablespoon lemon juice

1 tablespoon olive oil

1 tablespoon fresh dill, chopped

Salt and pepper to taste

NUTRITIONAL INFORMATION (per serving):

Calories: 390 • **Total Fat:** 28g • **Saturated Fat:** 12g • **Cholesterol:** 85mg • **Sodium:** 200mg • **Total Carbohydrates:** 6g • **Dietary Fiber:** 0g • **Sugars:** 3g • **Protein:** 28g

DIRECTIONS:

1. **Prepare the Lamb Mixture:** In a large bowl, combine the ground lamb, grated onion, minced garlic, parsley, mint, cumin, paprika, coriander, cinnamon, salt, and pepper. Mix until well combined, but avoid overworking the meat.

2. **Form the Kebabs:** Divide the lamb mixture into 8 equal portions. Mold each portion around a skewer into a long, sausage-like shape. Place the skewered koftas on a plate and chill in the refrigerator for at least 30 minutes to help them firm up.

3. **Make the Yogurt Sauce:** While the koftas are chilling, prepare the yogurt sauce. In a small bowl, whisk together the Greek yogurt, minced garlic, lemon juice, olive oil, chopped dill, salt, and pepper until smooth. Set aside in the refrigerator until ready to serve.

4. Preheat the air fryer to 400°F (200°C).

5. **Cook the Kofta Kebabs:**

   a. Place the chilled kofta kebabs in the air fryer basket, making sure they are not touching. You may need to cook in batches.

   b. Air fry for 10 minutes, turning halfway through, or until the koftas are browned on the outside and cooked through.

6. Serve the lamb kofta kebabs hot with the chilled yogurt sauce on the side.

Chapter 8

Appetizers and Snacks

Moroccan Air-Fried Spiced Carrot Fries

Yield: **4 servings** | Prep Time: **15 minutes** | Cook Time: **20 minutes**

INGREDIENTS:

1 pound carrots, peeled and cut into thin sticks

2 tablespoons olive oil

1 teaspoon ground cumin

1/2 teaspoon ground coriander

1/2 teaspoon smoked paprika

1/4 teaspoon ground cinnamon

1/4 teaspoon cayenne pepper (adjust to taste)

Salt and pepper to taste

Fresh cilantro, chopped for garnish

Optional: Lemon wedges for serving

NUTRITIONAL INFORMATION
(per serving):

Calories: 120 • Total Fat: 7g • Saturated Fat: 1g • Cholesterol: 0mg • Sodium: 125mg • Total Carbohydrates: 14g • Dietary Fiber: 4g • Sugars: 6g • Protein: 1g

DIRECTIONS:

1. In a large bowl, toss the carrot sticks with olive oil, ground cumin, ground coriander, smoked paprika, ground cinnamon, cayenne pepper, salt, and pepper until the carrots are evenly coated with the spices and oil.

2. Preheat the air fryer to 380°F (190°C).

3. Arrange the spiced carrot sticks in the air fryer basket in a single layer, making sure they are not overcrowded. You may need to cook in batches depending on the size of your air fryer.

4. Cook for 20 minutes, shaking the basket or turning the carrot fries halfway through until they are tender and crispy on the edges.

5. Once done, transfer the carrot fries to a serving dish and garnish with chopped fresh cilantro. Serve immediately with lemon wedges on the side, if desired.

Mediterranean Stuffed Mushrooms with Feta and Spinach

Yield: **12 stuffed mushrooms** | Prep Time: **15 minutes** | Cook Time: **10 minutes**

INGREDIENTS:

12 large cremini or button mushrooms, stems removed and finely chopped, caps intact

1 tablespoon olive oil, plus extra for brushing

1 small onion, finely diced

2 cloves garlic, minced

2 cups fresh spinach, roughly chopped

1/2 cup feta cheese, crumbled

1/4 cup breadcrumbs

1/4 teaspoon dried oregano

Salt and pepper to taste

Optional: 1 tablespoon pine nuts for a crunchy texture

Optional: Fresh parsley, chopped for garnish

NUTRITIONAL INFORMATION
(per stuffed mushroom):

Calories: 50 • Total Fat: 3g • Saturated Fat: 1g • Cholesterol: 5mg • Sodium: 100mg • Total Carbohydrates: 4g • Dietary Fiber: 1g • Sugars: 1g • Protein: 3g

DIRECTIONS:

1. Preheat the air fryer to 360°F (180°C).

2. Heat 1 tablespoon of olive oil in a skillet over medium heat. Sauté the diced onion and chopped mushroom stems until the onion is translucent and the moisture from the mushrooms has evaporated for about 5 minutes.

3. Add the minced garlic and chopped spinach to the skillet. Cook until the spinach is wilted, about 2 minutes. Remove from heat.

4. In a bowl, combine the sautéed vegetables with the crumbled feta cheese, breadcrumbs, dried oregano, salt, and pepper. Mix well. If using, stir in the pine nuts.

5. Brush the outside of the mushroom caps with olive oil. Stuff each mushroom cap generously with the spinach and feta mixture.

6. Arrange the stuffed mushrooms in a single layer in the air fryer basket. You may need to cook in batches depending on the size of your air fryer.

7. Cook for 10 minutes or until the mushrooms are tender and the tops are golden brown.

8. Serve the Mediterranean Stuffed Mushrooms warm, garnished with chopped fresh parsley if desired.

Mediterranean Air-Fried Artichoke Hearts with Garlic Aioli

Yield: *4 servings* | Prep Time: *15 minutes* | Cook Time: *10 minutes*

INGREDIENTS:

For Artichoke Hearts:

2 cans (14 oz each) artichoke hearts, drained and patted dry

2 tablespoons olive oil

1 teaspoon dried thyme

1/2 teaspoon paprika

Salt and pepper to taste

For Garlic Aioli:

1/2 cup mayonnaise

1 clove garlic, minced

1 tablespoon lemon juice

1/2 teaspoon Dijon mustard

Salt and pepper to taste

DIRECTIONS:

1. In a bowl, toss the drained artichoke hearts with olive oil, dried thyme, paprika, salt, and pepper until well coated.

2. Preheat the air fryer to 400°F (200°C).

3. Arrange the artichoke hearts in a single layer in the air fryer basket. You may need to cook in batches to avoid overcrowding.

4. Air fry for 10 minutes, or until the artichoke hearts are golden brown and crispy, shaking the basket halfway through cooking.

5. While the artichokes are cooking, prepare the garlic aioli. In a small bowl, mix together the mayonnaise, minced garlic, lemon juice, Dijon mustard, salt, and pepper until smooth.

6. Serve the air-fried artichoke hearts warm with the garlic aioli on the side for dipping.

NUTRITIONAL INFORMATION (per serving):

Calories: 280 • **Total Fat:** 24g • **Saturated Fat:** 3.5g • **Cholesterol:** 15mg • **Sodium:** 480mg • **Total Carbohydrates:** 14g • **Dietary Fiber:** 5g • **Sugars:** 2g • **Protein:** 3g

Egyptian Air-Fried Taameya (Fava Bean Falafel)

Yield: *18-20 falafel* | Prep Time: *20 minutes (plus soaking time for beans)* | Cook Time: *15 minutes*

INGREDIENTS:

1 cup dried split fava beans, soaked overnight

1/2 cup fresh parsley, roughly chopped

1/2 cup fresh cilantro, roughly chopped

1/2 cup fresh dill, roughly chopped

4 green onions, chopped

2 cloves garlic, minced

1 teaspoon ground cumin

1/2 teaspoon ground coriander

1/4 teaspoon cayenne pepper (adjust to taste)

Salt and pepper to taste

1 teaspoon baking powder

2 tablespoons sesame seeds

Olive oil spray (for air frying)

DIRECTIONS:

1. Drain the soaked fava beans and rinse them under cold water.

2. In a food processor, combine the soaked fava beans, parsley, cilantro, dill, green onions, garlic, cumin, coriander, cayenne pepper, salt, and pepper. Pulse until the mixture is finely ground but not pureed.

3. Transfer the mixture to a bowl and stir in the baking powder. Let the mixture sit for 10 minutes to allow the flavors to meld and the baking powder to activate.

4. Form the mixture into small patties about the size of a golf ball, then slightly flatten them. Sprinkle sesame seeds on both sides of each patty.

5. Preheat the air fryer to 375°F (190°C).

6. Spray the air fryer basket with olive oil spray. Place the taameya in the basket in a single layer, making sure they don't touch. Work in batches if necessary.

7. Spray the tops of the taameya lightly with olive oil. Air fry for 15 minutes, flipping halfway through, until they are golden brown and crispy.

8. Serve the air-fried taameya hot, with tahini sauce or yogurt for dipping.

NUTRITIONAL INFORMATION (per falafel):

Calories: 60 • **Total Fat:** 1.5g • **Saturated Fat:** 0.2g • **Cholesterol:** 0mg • **Sodium:** 100mg • **Total Carbohydrates:** 9g • **Dietary Fiber:** 2g • **Sugars:** 0.5g • **Protein:** 3g

Crispy Air-Fried Cauliflower with Tahini Dip

Yield: *4 servings* | Prep Time: *15 minutes* | Cook Time: *20 minutes*

INGREDIENTS:

For Air-Fried Cauliflower:

1 large head of cauliflower, cut into florets

2 tablespoons olive oil

1 teaspoon ground cumin

1/2 teaspoon smoked paprika

1/4 teaspoon garlic powder

Salt and pepper to taste

Olive oil spray (for air frying)

For Tahini Dip:

1/3 cup tahini (sesame seed paste)

1/4 cup water (adjust for desired consistency)

2 tablespoons lemon juice

1 clove garlic, minced

Salt to taste

Optional: 1 tablespoon chopped fresh parsley for garnish

Optional: Paprika for garnish

NUTRITIONAL INFORMATION
(per serving, including tahini dip):

Calories: 210 • **Total Fat:** 16g • **Saturated Fat:** 2g • **Cholesterol:** 0mg • **Sodium:** 150mg • **Total Carbohydrates:** 14g • **Dietary Fiber:** 5g • **Sugars:** 4g • **Protein:** 6g

DIRECTIONS:

1. In a large bowl, toss the cauliflower florets with olive oil, ground cumin, smoked paprika, garlic powder, salt, and pepper until well coated.

2. Preheat the air fryer to 400°F (200°C).

3. Arrange the seasoned cauliflower florets in the air fryer basket in a single layer, making sure they don't touch. Spray lightly with olive oil spray. You may need to cook in batches depending on the size of your air fryer.

4. Air fry for 20 minutes, or until the cauliflower is golden brown and crispy, shaking the basket halfway through cooking.

5. While the cauliflower is cooking, prepare the tahini dip. In a small bowl, whisk together tahini, water, lemon juice, minced garlic, and salt until smooth. Adjust the consistency with more water if needed.

6. Serve the crispy air-fried cauliflower hot, accompanied by the tahini dip. Garnish the dip with chopped parsley and a sprinkle of paprika if desired.

Air-Fried Pita Chips with Mediterranean Salsa

Yield: *4 servings* | Prep Time: *15 minutes* | Cook Time: *8 minutes*

INGREDIENTS:

For Air-Fried Pita Chips:

4 pita bread rounds

2 tablespoons olive oil

1/2 teaspoon garlic powder

Salt to taste

For Mediterranean Salsa:

1 cup cherry tomatoes, quartered

1/2 cup cucumber, diced

1/4 cup red onion, finely chopped

1/4 cup Kalamata olives, pitted and chopped

1/4 cup feta cheese, crumbled

2 tablespoons fresh parsley, chopped

1 tablespoon olive oil

1 tablespoon lemon juice

Salt and pepper to taste

NUTRITIONAL INFORMATION
((per serving):

Calories: 280 • **Total Fat:** 15g • **Saturated Fat:** 3g • **Cholesterol:** 8mg • **Sodium:** 400mg • **Total Carbohydrates:** 32g • **Dietary Fiber:** 2g • **Sugars:** 3g • **Protein:** 7g

DIRECTIONS:

1. Preheat the air fryer to 360°F (180°C).

2. Cut the pita bread into triangles or chip-sized pieces. In a large bowl, toss the pita pieces with olive oil, garlic powder, and salt until evenly coated.

3. Place the pita pieces in the air fryer basket in a single layer, ensuring they do not overlap. You may need to work in batches.

4. Air fry for 4 minutes, then flip the pita chips and continue air frying for another 4 minutes or until they are golden brown and crispy.

5. While the pita chips are cooking, prepare the Mediterranean salsa by combining cherry tomatoes, cucumber, red onion, Kalamata olives, feta cheese, and parsley in a mixing bowl.

6. Dress the salsa with olive oil and lemon juice. Season with salt and pepper to taste and gently mix to combine.

7. Once the pita chips are done, let them cool slightly before serving with the Mediterranean salsa on the side.

Greek-Style Air-Fried Zucchini Fritters

Yield: **12 fritters** | Prep Time: **20 minutes (including time for draining zucchini)** | Cook Time: **10 minutes**

INGREDIENTS:

2 medium zucchinis, grated

1 teaspoon salt (for draining zucchini)

2 large eggs, beaten

1/2 cup feta cheese, crumbled

1/4 cup fresh dill, chopped

1/4 cup scallions, chopped

1/2 cup all-purpose flour

1 teaspoon baking powder

1/2 teaspoon black pepper

Olive oil spray (for air frying)

Optional: Lemon wedges and Greek yogurt or tzatziki for serving

NUTRITIONAL INFORMATION
(per fritter):

Calories: 60 • **Total Fat:** 2g • **Saturated Fat:** 1g • **Cholesterol:** 30mg • **Sodium:** 200mg • **Total Carbohydrates:** 7g • **Dietary Fiber:** 1g • **Sugars:** 1g • **Protein:** 3g

DIRECTIONS:

1. Place the grated zucchini in a colander and sprinkle with 1 teaspoon of salt. Let it sit for 10 minutes to draw out moisture. Squeeze the zucchini to remove as much water as possible.

2. In a large bowl, combine the drained zucchini, beaten eggs, crumbled feta cheese, chopped dill, chopped scallions, all-purpose flour, baking powder, and black pepper. Stir until the mixture is well combined.

3. Preheat the air fryer to 375°F (190°C).

4. Form the zucchini mixture into small patties, about 2-3 inches in diameter.

5. Spray the air fryer basket with olive oil spray. Place the fritters in the basket, making sure they don't touch. You may need to cook in batches.

6. Spray the tops of the fritters lightly with olive oil. Cook in the air fryer for 5 minutes, then flip the fritters and continue to cook for another 5 minutes or until they are golden brown and crispy.

7. Serve the Greek-style zucchini fritters warm with lemon wedges and Greek yogurt or tzatziki sauce, if desired.

Turkish Air-Fried Sigara Böreği (Cheese-Stuffed Pastry Rolls)

Yield: **15 rolls** | Prep Time: **20 minutes** | Cook Time: **10 minutes**

INGREDIENTS:

15 sheets of phyllo dough, cut into 5-inch squares

1 cup feta cheese, crumbled

1/2 cup mozzarella cheese, grated

1 tablespoon fresh parsley, chopped

1 egg, beaten (reserve a little for brushing)

1/4 teaspoon black pepper

Olive oil spray (for air frying)

Optional: 1 tablespoon dill or mint for a different flavor profile

NUTRITIONAL INFORMATION
(per roll):

Calories: 120 • **Total Fat:** 6g • **Saturated Fat:** 3g • **Cholesterol:** 25mg • **Sodium:** 250mg • **Total Carbohydrates:** 10g • **Dietary Fiber:** 0g • **Sugars:** 1g • **Protein:** 5g

DIRECTIONS:

1. In a bowl, mix together the crumbled feta cheese, grated mozzarella cheese, chopped parsley, beaten egg (reserving a bit for brushing the phyllo), and black pepper. Add dill or mint if using, and combine well.

2. Lay a phyllo square flat on a clean surface. Place a tablespoon of the cheese mixture near the bottom edge of the square.

3. Fold the sides of the phyllo in over the filling, then roll up from the bottom to form a tight cigar shape. Brush the edge with a little beaten egg to seal. Repeat with the remaining phyllo squares and filling.

4. Preheat the air fryer to 360°F (180°C).

5. Spray the air fryer basket with olive oil spray. Place the Sigara Böreği in the basket in a single layer, making sure they don't touch. You may need to cook in batches.

6. Spray the tops of the Sigara Böreği lightly with olive oil. Air fry for 10 minutes or until golden brown and crispy, turning halfway through the cooking time.

7. Serve the Air-Fried Sigara Böreği warm as an appetizer or snack.

Crispy Air-Fried Falafel Balls

Yield: *20 falafel balls* | Prep Time: *20 minutes (plus soaking time for chickpeas)* | Cook Time: *15 minutes*

INGREDIENTS:

1 cup dried chickpeas, soaked overnight (do not use canned chickpeas)

1/2 large onion, roughly chopped

2 cloves garlic, minced

1 cup fresh parsley, roughly chopped

1 cup fresh cilantro, roughly chopped

1 teaspoon ground cumin

1 teaspoon ground coriander

1/2 teaspoon chili powder

1/2 teaspoon baking soda

Salt and pepper to taste

2 tablespoons all-purpose flour (or chickpea flour for gluten-free option)

Olive oil spray (for air frying)

**NUTRITIONAL INFORMATION
(per falafel ball):**

Calories: 60 • **Total Fat:** 1g • **Saturated Fat:** 0g • **Cholesterol:** 0mg • **Sodium:** 80mg • **Total Carbohydrates:** 10g • **Dietary Fiber:** 2g • **Sugars:** 2g • **Protein:** 3g

DIRECTIONS:

1. Drain and rinse the soaked chickpeas thoroughly. Pat them dry.

2. In a food processor, combine the chickpeas, onion, garlic, parsley, cilantro, cumin, coriander, chili powder, and baking soda. Pulse until the mixture is finely ground but not pureed.

3. Transfer the mixture to a bowl. Season with salt and pepper. Stir in the flour until the mixture can be shaped into small balls. If the mixture is too wet, add a little more flour.

4. Form the mixture into small balls about the size of a walnut.

5. Preheat the air fryer to 375°F (190°C).

6. Spray the air fryer basket with olive oil spray. Place the falafel balls in the basket, making sure they don't touch. Work in batches if necessary.

7. Spray the falafel balls lightly with olive oil. Cook in the air fryer for 15 minutes, turning halfway through, until they are golden and crispy.

8. Serve the falafel hot with your choice of dipping sauce, like tahini or tzatziki.

Air-Fried Eggplant Parmesan Bites

Yield: *4 servings* | Prep Time: *20 minutes* | Cook Time: *15 minutes*

INGREDIENTS:

1 medium eggplant, cut into 1/2-inch cubes

1 cup all-purpose flour

2 large eggs, beaten

1 cup breadcrumbs

1/2 cup grated Parmesan cheese

1 teaspoon dried oregano

1/2 teaspoon garlic powder

Salt and pepper to taste

Olive oil spray (for air frying)

1 cup marinara sauce, warmed (for dipping)

Fresh basil leaves, for garnish

**NUTRITIONAL INFORMATION
(per serving):**

Calories: 280 • **Total Fat:** 7g • **Saturated Fat:** 3g • **Cholesterol:** 95mg • **Sodium:** 500mg • **Total Carbohydrates:** 42g • **Dietary Fiber:** 5g • **Sugars:** 8g • **Protein:** 13g

DIRECTIONS:

1. In a shallow bowl, mix together the breadcrumbs, grated Parmesan cheese, dried oregano, garlic powder, salt, and pepper.

2. Dredge the eggplant cubes in flour, shaking off the excess. Dip them into the beaten eggs, then coat them in the breadcrumb mixture.

3. Preheat the air fryer to 390°F (200°C).

4. Spray the air fryer basket with olive oil spray. Arrange the eggplant cubes in a single layer in the basket, making sure they do not touch. Work in batches if necessary.

5. Spray the eggplant cubes lightly with olive oil spray. Air fry for about 15 minutes or until golden brown and crispy, shaking the basket halfway through cooking.

6. Serve the Air-Fried Eggplant Parmesan Bites warm, garnished with fresh basil leaves and accompanied by warm marinara sauce for dipping.

Crispy Air-Fried Chickpeas with Za'atar Seasoning

Yield: *4 servings* | Prep Time: *5 minutes* | Cook Time: *15 minutes*

INGREDIENTS:

2 cans (15 oz each) chickpeas, drained, rinsed, and patted dry

2 tablespoons olive oil

2 tablespoons za'atar seasoning

1/2 teaspoon salt (adjust to taste)

Optional: Pinch of cayenne pepper for extra heat

NUTRITIONAL INFORMATION (per serving):

Calories: 210 • **Total Fat:** 8g • **Saturated Fat:** 1g • **Cholesterol:** 0mg • **Sodium:** 300mg • **Total Carbohydrates:** 27g • **Dietary Fiber:** 8g • **Sugars:** 0g • **Protein:** 10g

DIRECTIONS:

1. Preheat the air fryer to 390°F (200°C).

2. In a large bowl, toss the dried chickpeas with olive oil, za'atar seasoning, salt, and optional cayenne pepper until evenly coated.

3. Spread the chickpeas in a single layer in the air fryer basket. You may need to cook in batches to avoid overcrowding for even crispiness.

4. Air fry for about 15 minutes, shaking the basket halfway through the cooking time until the chickpeas are golden brown and crispy.

5. Remove the chickpeas from the air fryer and let them cool slightly. They will continue to crisp up as they cool.

6. Serve the crispy air-fried chickpeas as a snack or as a topping for salads or soups.

Air-Fried Feta-Stuffed Peppers

Yield: *8 stuffed peppers* | Prep Time: *15 minutes* | Cook Time: *10 minutes*

INGREDIENTS:

8 mini bell peppers, halved and seeds removed

1 cup feta cheese, crumbled

1/4 cup cream cheese, softened

1 tablespoon olive oil

1 clove garlic, minced

1 teaspoon dried oregano

1 teaspoon dried basil

Salt and pepper to taste

Optional: Fresh parsley or basil for garnish

Optional: Drizzle of balsamic glaze for serving

NUTRITIONAL INFORMATION (per stuffed pepper):

Calories: 90 • **Total Fat:** 7g • **Saturated Fat:** 4g • **Cholesterol:** 25mg • **Sodium:** 200mg • **Total Carbohydrates:** 3g • **Dietary Fiber:** 1g • **Sugars:** 2g • **Protein:** 4g

DIRECTIONS:

1. In a mixing bowl, combine the crumbled feta cheese, softened cream cheese, olive oil, minced garlic, dried oregano, dried basil, salt, and pepper. Mix until well combined and smooth.

2. Carefully stuff each halved mini bell pepper with the feta cheese mixture, pressing it in to fill the cavity.

3. Preheat the air fryer to 370°F (190°C).

4. Arrange the stuffed peppers in the air fryer basket in a single layer cut side up. Depending on the size of your air fryer, you may need to work in batches.

5. Air fry for 10 minutes or until the peppers are tender and the cheese filling is slightly golden.

6. Carefully remove the stuffed peppers from the air fryer and place them on a serving platter.

7. Garnish with fresh parsley or basil if using, and optionally drizzle with balsamic glaze before serving.

8. Serve warm as a delicious and colorful appetizer or side dish.

Air-Fried Halloumi Cheese Sticks with Honey Drizzle

Yield: *4 servings* | Prep Time: *10 minutes* | Cook Time: *8 minutes*

INGREDIENTS:

8 oz halloumi cheese, cut into 1/2-inch thick sticks

1/4 cup all-purpose flour

1 large egg, beaten

1/2 cup breadcrumbs

1 teaspoon dried oregano

Olive oil spray (for air frying)

1/4 cup honey, for drizzling

Optional: Sesame seeds or crushed pistachios for garnish

NUTRITIONAL INFORMATION (per serving):

Calories: 320 • **Total Fat:** 18g • **Saturated Fat:** 11g • **Cholesterol:** 60mg • **Sodium:** 800mg • **Total Carbohydrates:** 26g • **Dietary Fiber:** 1g • **Sugars:** 12g (includes 11g added sugars from honey) • **Protein:** 15g

DIRECTIONS:

1. Preheat the air fryer to 400°F (200°C).

2. **Set up three shallow bowls for breading:** one with flour, one with the beaten egg, and one with breadcrumbs mixed with dried oregano.

3. Dredge each halloumi stick in flour, tapping off the excess. Dip in the beaten egg, then coat with the seasoned breadcrumbs.

4. Spray the air fryer basket with olive oil spray. Arrange the breaded halloumi sticks in the basket in a single layer, making sure they don't touch. You may need to work in batches depending on the size of your air fryer.

5. Spray the tops of the halloumi sticks lightly with olive oil. Air fry for 8 minutes, turning halfway through, until golden brown and crispy.

6. Warm the honey in a microwave-safe dish for about 20 seconds or until it becomes runny.

7. Arrange the air-fried halloumi sticks on a serving plate. Drizzle with warm honey and sprinkle with sesame seeds or crushed pistachios if using.

8. Serve immediately while the halloumi sticks are warm and crispy.

Air-Fried Caprese Skewers (Tomato, Basil, and Mozzarella)

Yield: *8 skewers* | Prep Time: *15 minutes* | Cook Time: *2 minutes*

INGREDIENTS:

16 cherry tomatoes

16 small fresh mozzarella balls (bocconcini)

16 fresh basil leaves

8 wooden skewers

2 tablespoons olive oil

Salt and pepper to taste

Balsamic glaze for drizzling

NUTRITIONAL INFORMATION (per skewer):

Calories: 100 • **Total Fat:** 8g • **Saturated Fat:** 3g • **Cholesterol:** 15mg • **Sodium:** 200mg • **Total Carbohydrates:** 2g • **Dietary Fiber:** 0g • **Sugars:** 1g • **Protein:** 6g

DIRECTIONS:

1. If using wooden skewers, soak them in water for at least 30 minutes before assembling to prevent burning.

2. Thread each skewer with a cherry tomato, a fresh basil leaf, and a mozzarella ball. Repeat the pattern to have 2 of each ingredient per skewer.

3. Preheat the air fryer to 360°F (180°C).

4. Arrange the skewers in the air fryer basket, making sure they do not touch each other. You may need to work in batches depending on the size of your air fryer.

5. Lightly brush the skewers with olive oil and season with salt and pepper.

6. Air fry for 2 minutes, just enough to warm the ingredients through. The goal is not to cook the skewers but to slightly melt the mozzarella and intensify the flavors.

7. Carefully remove the skewers from the air fryer. Drizzle with balsamic glaze before serving.

8. Serve immediately while warm.

Lebanese Air-Fried Kibbeh Balls (Meat and Bulgur Wheat Croquettes)

Yield: **20 kibbeh balls** | Prep Time: **30 minutes** | Cook Time: **15 minutes**

INGREDIENTS:

1 cup fine bulgur wheat

1/2 pound ground beef or lamb (lean)

1 small onion, finely chopped

1/2 cup fresh parsley, finely chopped

1 teaspoon ground cumin

1/2 teaspoon ground allspice

1/2 teaspoon ground cinnamon

Salt and pepper to taste

1/4 cup pine nuts (optional)

Olive oil spray (for air frying)

For the Filling:

1/2 pound ground beef or lamb

1 small onion, finely diced

1 teaspoon ground allspice

Salt and pepper to taste

1/4 cup pine nuts, toasted

DIRECTIONS:

1. Soak the bulgur wheat in cold water for 30 minutes. Drain well, squeezing out excess water.

2. In a large bowl, mix the soaked bulgur, 1/2 pound of ground meat, chopped onion, parsley, cumin, allspice, cinnamon, salt, and pepper. Knead the mixture with your hands until well combined. If using, stir in 1/4 cup of pine nuts.

3. To prepare the filling, cook the other 1/2 pound of ground meat in a skillet over medium heat with the diced onion, allspice, salt, and pepper. Cook until the meat is browned and the onion is soft. Stir in the toasted pine nuts and set aside to cool.

4. Take a small amount of the bulgur and meat dough and form it into a ball about the size of a walnut. Make an indentation in the center of each ball with your finger, and fill it with a teaspoon of the meat filling. Close the dough around the filling and shape it into an oval or football shape. Repeat with the remaining dough and filling.

5. Preheat the air fryer to 350°F (175°C).

6. Spray the air fryer basket with olive oil spray. Place the kibbeh balls in the basket, making sure they don't touch. Spray the kibbeh balls lightly with olive oil.

7. Air fry for about 15 minutes, turning halfway through until they are golden brown and cooked through.

8. Serve the air-fried kibbeh balls hot, with yogurt or tahini sauce for dipping.

NUTRITIONAL INFORMATION
(per kibbeh ball):

Calories: 120 • **Total Fat:** 6g • **Saturated Fat:** 2g • **Cholesterol:** 20mg • **Sodium:** 60mg • **Total Carbohydrates:** 8g • **Dietary Fiber:** 2g • **Sugars:** 0g • **Protein:** 8g

Chapter 9

Desserts

Air-Fried Chocolate and Hazelnut Brik

Yield: *8 briks* | Prep Time: *20 minutes* | Cook Time: *8 minutes*

INGREDIENTS:

8 sheets of brik pastry (or phyllo dough if brik is unavailable)

1/2 cup chocolate hazelnut spread (e.g., Nutella)

1/2 cup chopped hazelnuts, toasted

2 tablespoons unsalted butter, melted

Powdered sugar, for dusting

Olive oil spray (for air frying)

NUTRITIONAL INFORMATION (per brik):

Calories: 250 • **Total Fat:** 15g • **Saturated Fat:** 4g • **Cholesterol:** 8mg • **Sodium:** 120mg • **Total Carbohydrates:** 25g • **Dietary Fiber:** 2g • **Sugars:** 12g • **Protein:** 4g

DIRECTIONS:

1. **Prep the Pastry:** If using phyllo dough, stack two sheets together for each brik, brushing lightly with melted butter between the layers, to ensure strength for holding the filling.

2. **Assemble the Briks:**

   a. Lay out one sheet of brik pastry (or your doubled-up phyllo sheets) on a clean work surface. Place a tablespoon of chocolate hazelnut spread in the center and sprinkle with toasted chopped hazelnuts.

   b. Fold the pastry over the filling to create a triangle or square shape, pressing the edges to seal. Brush the outside lightly with melted butter. Repeat with the remaining pastry sheets and filling.

3. Preheat the air fryer to 350°F (180°C).

4. **Air Fry the Briks:**

   a. Lightly spray the air fryer basket with olive oil spray. Place the prepared briks in the basket, ensuring they do not touch. You may need to cook in batches.

   b. Air fry for 6-8 minutes, or until the briks are golden and crispy, flipping halfway through the cooking time.

5. Allow the briks to cool slightly on a wire rack. Dust with powdered sugar before serving.

Air-Fried Apple and Cinnamon Bourekas

Yield: *8 bourekas* | Prep Time: *20 minutes* | Cook Time: *15 minutes*

INGREDIENTS:

1 package (1 pound) puff pastry, thawed

2 medium apples, peeled, cored, and finely chopped

1/4 cup granulated sugar

1 teaspoon ground cinnamon

1 tablespoon lemon juice

1 egg, beaten (for egg wash)

Powdered sugar for dusting (optional)

NUTRITIONAL INFORMATION (per boureka):

Calories: 300 • **Total Fat:** 18g • **Saturated Fat:** 5g • **Cholesterol:** 20mg • **Sodium:** 150mg • **Total Carbohydrates:** 32g • **Dietary Fiber:** 2g • **Sugars:** 10g • **Protein:** 4g

DIRECTIONS:

1. **Prepare the Apple Filling:** In a medium bowl, combine the chopped apples with granulated sugar, ground cinnamon, and lemon juice. Mix well until the apples are evenly coated with the sugar and spices.

2. Preheat the air fryer to 360°F (180°C).

3. **Prepare the Puff Pastry:** Roll out the puff pastry on a lightly floured surface to smooth out any creases. Cut the pastry into 8 equal squares.

4. **Assemble the Bourekas:** Spoon a heaping tablespoon of the apple filling into the center of each puff pastry square. Fold the pastry over the filling to form a triangle, pressing the edges to seal. Use a fork to crimp the edges for a better seal.

5. **Apply Egg Wash:** Lightly brush the top of each boureka with the beaten egg. This will give them a nice golden color when air-fried.

6. **Air Fry the Bourekas:**

   a. Place the bourekas in the air fryer basket in a single layer, ensuring they are not touching. You may need to cook them in batches.

   b. Air fry for 12-15 minutes or until the bourekas are puffed up and golden brown.

7. **Serve:** Let the bourekas cool slightly before dusting with powdered sugar if desired. Serve warm as a delicious dessert or snack.

Lemon and Herb Ricotta Stuffed Air-Fried Peaches

Yield: *4 servings (2 halves per serving)* | Prep Time: *15 minutes* | Cook Time: *8 minutes*

INGREDIENTS:

4 ripe peaches, halved and pitted
1 cup ricotta cheese
2 tablespoons honey, plus extra for drizzling
Zest of 1 lemon
1 tablespoon lemon juice
2 tablespoons fresh basil, finely chopped
2 tablespoons fresh mint, finely chopped
Olive oil spray
Optional for garnish: additional basil or mint leaves, chopped nuts

NUTRITIONAL INFORMATION (per serving):

Calories: 200 • **Total Fat:** 8g • **Saturated Fat:** 5g • **Cholesterol:** 30mg • **Sodium:** 80mg • **Total Carbohydrates:** 26g • **Dietary Fiber:** 2g • **Sugars:** 22g (includes added sugars from honey) • **Protein:** 8g

DIRECTIONS:

1. **Prepare the Filling:** In a mixing bowl, combine the ricotta cheese, honey, lemon zest, lemon juice, chopped basil, and mint. Stir until the mixture is smooth and well combined.

2. **Stuff the Peaches:** Using a spoon, carefully fill the cavity of each peach half with the ricotta mixture. The amount of filling will depend on the size of the peaches but aim to use about 2 tablespoons per half.

3. Preheat the air fryer to 375°F (190°C).

4. **Air Fry the Peaches:**

   a. Lightly spray the air fryer basket with olive oil spray to prevent sticking. Place the stuffed peach halves in the basket, cut side up, ensuring they are not touching.

   b. Air fry for 6-8 minutes, or until the peaches are tender and the ricotta filling is slightly golden.

5. **Serve:** Carefully remove the peach halves from the air fryer and arrange them on a serving plate. Drizzle with additional honey and garnish with extra basil, mint, or chopped nuts if desired. Serve warm as a delicious and healthy dessert.

Air-Fried Almond and Orange Florentines

Yield: *12 Florentines* | Prep Time: *15 minutes* | Cook Time: *6 minutes*

INGREDIENTS:

1 cup sliced almonds
1/4 cup all-purpose flour
1/3 cup sugar
1/4 cup butter
1/4 cup heavy cream
2 tablespoons honey
Zest of 1 orange
1/2 teaspoon vanilla extract
Pinch of salt
4 ounces dark chocolate, melted (for drizzling)

DIRECTIONS:

1. **Combine Dry Ingredients:** In a bowl, mix together the sliced almonds, all-purpose flour, and a pinch of salt. Stir in the orange zest.

2. **Prepare the Caramel Mixture:** In a saucepan over medium heat, combine the sugar, butter, heavy cream, and honey. Cook, stirring constantly, until the mixture comes to a boil. Let it boil for 1 minute, then remove from heat.

3. **Mix and Let Cool:** Pour the caramel mixture over the almond mixture and stir until well combined. Add the vanilla extract and mix. Let the mixture cool slightly; it should still be pliable but not too hot to handle.

4. Preheat the air fryer to 350°F (180°C).

5. **Shape the Florentines:** Place spoonfuls of the mixture onto a parchment paper-lined air fryer basket, leaving ample space between each as they will spread. You may need to work in batches depending on the size of your air fryer.

6. Air fry for 5-6 minutes or until the edges are golden brown. Watch closely to prevent burning.

NUTRITIONAL INFORMATION
(per Florentine, approximate):

Calories: 180 • Total Fat: 12g •
Saturated Fat: 5g • Cholesterol: 15mg •
Sodium: 20mg • Total Carbohydrates:
17g • Dietary Fiber: 2g • Sugars: 14g •
Protein: 3g

7. **Cool:** Allow the Florentines to cool completely in the basket or on a wire rack. They will crisp up as they cool.

8. **Decorate with Chocolate:** Once cooled, drizzle the Florentines with melted dark chocolate. Allow the chocolate to set before serving.

9. **Serve:** Enjoy these crunchy, nutty treats as a delicious snack or dessert.

Honey-Lemon Air-Fried Doughnuts

Yield: **8 doughnuts** | Prep Time: **20 minutes** | Cook Time: **10 minutes**

INGREDIENTS:

For the Doughnuts:

1 cup all-purpose flour

1/3 cup granulated sugar

1 teaspoon baking powder

1/2 teaspoon salt

1/2 teaspoon lemon zest

1/4 cup milk

1/4 cup Greek yogurt

1 tablespoon lemon juice

1 egg

2 tablespoons unsalted butter, melted

For the Honey-Lemon Glaze:

1/2 cup powdered sugar

2 tablespoons honey

2 tablespoons lemon juice

Extra lemon zest for garnish

NUTRITIONAL INFORMATION
(per doughnut):

Calories: 180 • Total Fat: 4g • Saturated
Fat: 2g • Cholesterol: 30mg • Sodium:
160mg • Total Carbohydrates: 34g
• Dietary Fiber: 0.5g • Sugars: 20g •
Protein: 3g

DIRECTIONS:

1. **Make the Doughnut Batter:**

   a. In a large mixing bowl, whisk together the flour, granulated sugar, baking powder, salt, and lemon zest.

   b. In a separate bowl, mix the milk, Greek yogurt, lemon juice, egg, and melted butter until well combined.

   c. Pour the wet ingredients into the dry ingredients and stir until just combined. Be careful not to overmix.

2. Preheat the air fryer to 350°F (180°C). Grease the air fryer basket or use parchment paper with holes to prevent sticking.

3. **Form the Doughnuts:** Transfer the dough to a piping bag or a zip-top bag with a corner cut-off. Pipe the dough into doughnut shapes on the greased air fryer basket or parchment. If you have a doughnut pan that fits in your air fryer, you can use that instead.

4. Air fry the doughnuts for 5 minutes, then flip and air fry for another 4-5 minutes or until golden and cooked through.

5. **Prepare the Honey-Lemon Glaze:** While the doughnuts are cooking, prepare the glaze by whisking together the powdered sugar, honey, and lemon juice in a bowl until smooth.

6. **Glaze the Doughnuts:** Once the doughnuts are done and slightly cooled, dip each doughnut into the honey-lemon glaze, ensuring both sides are well coated. Place on a wire rack to let any excess glaze drip off. Sprinkle with extra lemon zest for garnish.

7. Serve the doughnuts warm or at room temperature for a delightful treat.

Greek Yogurt and Honey Puffs

Yield: *15 puffs* | Prep Time: *15 minutes* | Cook Time: *10 minutes*

INGREDIENTS:

1 cup all-purpose flour

2 teaspoons baking powder

1/4 teaspoon salt

2 tablespoons sugar

1 cup Greek yogurt

2 large eggs

1 teaspoon vanilla extract

Zest of 1 lemon

Olive oil spray (for air frying)

Honey, for drizzling

Powdered sugar, for dusting

Optional: Chopped nuts or fresh berries for garnish

NUTRITIONAL INFORMATION (per puff):

Calories: 70 • **Total Fat:** 1g • **Saturated Fat:** 0g • **Cholesterol:** 25mg • **Sodium:** 85mg • **Total Carbohydrates:** 11g • **Dietary Fiber:** 0g • **Sugars:** 4g (includes honey drizzle) • **Protein:** 3g

DIRECTIONS:

1. **Prepare the Batter:**

   a. In a large mixing bowl, whisk together the flour, baking powder, salt, and sugar.

   b. In another bowl, mix the Greek yogurt, eggs, vanilla extract, and lemon zest until well combined.

   c. Fold the wet ingredients into the dry ingredients until just combined. Be careful not to overmix.

2. Preheat the air fryer to 350°F (180°C).

3. **Shape the Puffs:** Lightly grease your hands with olive oil. Take a tablespoon of the batter and roll it into a ball. Repeat with the remaining batter. You should have about 15 puffs.

4. **Air Fry the Puffs:**

   a. Lightly spray the air fryer basket with olive oil spray. Place the puffs in the basket, making sure they are not touching. You may need to cook them in batches.

   b. Air fry for 8-10 minutes or until the puffs are golden brown and cooked through.

5. **Serve:** Drizzle the warm puffs with honey and dust with powdered sugar. Garnish with chopped nuts or fresh berries if desired. Serve immediately.

Rose Water and Pistachio Air-Fried Pastry Twists

Yield: *12 twists* | Prep Time: *20 minutes* | Cook Time: *10 minutes*

INGREDIENTS:

1 package of puff pastry (about 1 pound), thawed

1/2 cup granulated sugar

1 tablespoon rose water

1/2 cup finely chopped pistachios

1 egg, beaten (for egg wash)

Powdered sugar, for dusting (optional)

DIRECTIONS:

1. **Prepare the Puff Pastry:** Roll out the puff pastry on a lightly floured surface into a rectangle about 1/4-inch thick. Cut the pastry into 12 strips, approximately 1 inch wide and 6 inches long.

2. **Flavor the Sugar:** In a small bowl, mix the granulated sugar with the rose water until well combined. The sugar should be slightly damp.

3. **Add Pistachios:** Spread the rose water sugar evenly over the surface of each pastry strip. Then, sprinkle the finely chopped pistachios on top of the sugar.

4. **Form the Twists:** Gently twist each strip several times to create a spiral shape. Press the ends slightly to ensure they don't unravel during cooking.

5. Preheat the air fryer to 375°F (190°C).

6. **Egg Wash:** Brush each twist lightly with the beaten egg. This will give the pastry a golden color and help seal any loose ends.

7. **Air Fry:**

   a. Place the pastry twists in the air fryer basket in a single layer, ensuring they do not touch. You may need to cook them in batches.

   b. Air fry for 8-10 minutes or until the twists are golden brown and puffed up.

8. **Serve:** Allow the twists to cool slightly on a wire rack. Dust with powdered sugar if desired before serving.

Air-Fried Baklava Bites

Yield: **24 bites** | Prep Time: **20 minutes** | Cook Time: **10 minutes**

INGREDIENTS:

1 package phyllo dough, thawed
1 cup walnuts, finely chopped
1/2 cup almonds, finely chopped
1/4 cup sugar
1 teaspoon ground cinnamon
1/2 cup unsalted butter, melted

For the Syrup:
1/2 cup water
1/2 cup sugar
1/4 cup honey
1 tablespoon lemon juice
1 cinnamon stick

DIRECTIONS:

1. **Prepare the Filling:** In a bowl, mix together the walnuts, almonds, sugar, and ground cinnamon. Set aside.

2. **Prepare the Phyllo Dough:** Carefully unroll the phyllo dough. Cover with a damp cloth to prevent it from drying out. Take one sheet, brush it lightly with melted butter, and place another sheet on top. Repeat the buttering and layering until you have 4 layers.

3. **Assemble the Baklava Bites:** Cut the layered phyllo dough into 3-inch squares. Place about 1 teaspoon of the nut mixture in the center of each square. Fold the edges over to form a parcel or bite, ensuring the filling is securely enclosed. Brush the outside with a little more melted butter.

4. Preheat the air fryer to 350°F (180°C).

5. **Air Fry the Baklava Bites:**

   a. Place the baklava bites in the air fryer basket, ensuring they don't touch. Depending on the size of your air fryer, you may need to cook them in batches.

   b. Air fry for 8-10 minutes or until golden and crispy.

6. **Prepare the Syrup:** While the baklava bites are air frying, combine water, sugar, honey, lemon juice, and a cinnamon stick in a small saucepan. Bring to a boil, then reduce heat and simmer for about 10 minutes until the syrup thickens slightly. Remove the cinnamon stick.

7. **Finish the Baklava Bites:** Once the baklava bites are cooked, immediately drizzle the warm syrup over the hot baklava bites. Allow them to soak up the syrup for a few minutes before serving.

8. Serve the baklava bites warm or at room temperature as a delicious dessert.

Cinnamon and Sugar Air-Fried Churros with Chocolate Sauce

Yield: **20 churros** | Prep Time: **25 minutes** | Cook Time: **10 minutes**

INGREDIENTS:

For the Churros:

1 cup water

1/3 cup unsalted butter

2 tablespoons granulated sugar

1/4 teaspoon salt

1 cup all-purpose flour

1 teaspoon vanilla extract

2 large eggs

Olive oil spray

For the Cinnamon Sugar Coating:

1/2 cup granulated sugar

1 teaspoon ground cinnamon

For the Chocolate Sauce:

1/2 cup heavy cream

1 cup dark chocolate chips or chopped dark chocolate

1 tablespoon unsalted butter

NUTRITIONAL INFORMATION
(per churro, not including chocolate sauce):

Calories: 120 • Total Fat: 6g • Saturated Fat: 3.5g • Cholesterol: 30mg • Sodium: 45mg • Total Carbohydrates: 14g • Dietary Fiber: 0.5g • Sugars: 7g • Protein: 2g

DIRECTIONS:

1. **Prepare the Churro Dough:**

   a. In a medium saucepan, combine water, butter, sugar, and salt. Bring to a boil over medium heat. Reduce heat to low, add flour all at once, and stir vigorously until the mixture forms a ball, about 1 minute. Remove from heat.

   b. Stir in vanilla. Add eggs one at a time, stirring well after each addition, until the dough becomes smooth.

2. Preheat the air fryer to 370°F (190°C).

3. **Pipe the Churros:** Transfer the churro dough to a piping bag fitted with a large star tip. Pipe the dough into 4-inch lengths on a parchment-lined surface, cutting the ends with scissors.

4. **Air Fry the Churros:**

   a. Lightly spray the air fryer basket with olive oil spray. Place the churros in the basket, making sure they are not touching. You may need to cook them in batches.

   b. Air fry for 9-10 minutes or until golden brown. Carefully remove them and let them cool slightly.

5. **Coat the Churros:** Mix the sugar and cinnamon in a shallow dish. Roll the warm churros in the cinnamon sugar mixture until well coated.

6. **Make the Chocolate Sauce:** Heat the heavy cream in a small saucepan over medium heat until it begins to simmer. Remove from heat and add the chocolate chips and butter. Let sit for 1 minute, then stir until smooth and glossy.

7. Serve the air-fried churros warm with the chocolate sauce for dipping.

Air-Fried Ricotta and Orange Zest Cannoli

Yield: **8 cannoli** | Prep Time: **30 minutes (includes dough rest time)** | Cook Time: **10 minutes**

INGREDIENTS:

For the Cannoli Shells:

1 cup all-purpose flour

2 tablespoons sugar

1/2 teaspoon ground cinnamon

1 tablespoon unsalted butter, melted

2-3 tablespoons white wine or water

Olive oil spray (for air frying)

DIRECTIONS:

1. **Make the Cannoli Dough:** In a mixing bowl, combine the flour, sugar, and cinnamon. Add the melted butter and gradually add the white wine or water, mixing until a dough forms. Knead the dough on a lightly floured surface until smooth. Wrap it in plastic wrap and let it rest for 20 minutes.

2. **Roll Out the Dough:** After resting, divide the dough into 8 equal pieces. Roll each piece out on a lightly floured surface into a thin oval shape, large enough to wrap around your cannoli tubes.

For the Filling:

1 cup ricotta cheese, strained

1/4 cup powdered sugar, plus extra for dusting

Zest of 1 orange

1/4 teaspoon vanilla extract

2 tablespoons mini chocolate chips

Additional:

Cannoli tubes (for shaping)

NUTRITIONAL INFORMATION
(per cannoli):

Calories: 180 • **Total Fat:** 8g • **Saturated Fat:** 5g • **Cholesterol:** 20mg • **Sodium:** 45mg • **Total Carbohydrates:** 22g • **Dietary Fiber:** 0.5g • **Sugars:** 10g • **Protein:** 6g

3. **Wrap and Air Fry:**

   a. Lightly spray the cannoli tubes with olive oil spray. Wrap the dough ovals around the tubes, sealing the edges with a little water.

   b. Preheat the air fryer to 360°F (180°C).

   c. Place the wrapped cannoli tubes in the air fryer basket, ensuring they are not touching. Air fry for 8-10 minutes or until golden and crispy. Turn the tubes halfway through cooking. Allow to cool before gently sliding the shells off the tubes.

4. **Prepare the Filling:** In a bowl, mix the ricotta cheese, powdered sugar, orange zest, and vanilla extract until smooth. Fold in the mini chocolate chips.

5. **Fill the Cannoli:** Once the shells have cooled, use a piping bag to fill them with the ricotta mixture. If you don't have a piping bag, a zip-top bag with the cut-off corner also works.

6. **Serve:** Dust the filled cannoli with powdered sugar before serving. Enjoy fresh for the best texture.

Air-Fried Semolina and Coconut Cake with Syrup

Yield: *8 servings* | Prep Time: *15 minutes* | Cook Time: *20 minutes*

INGREDIENTS:

For the Cake:

1 cup semolina

1/2 cup desiccated coconut

1/2 cup granulated sugar

1 teaspoon baking powder

1/2 cup plain yogurt

1/4 cup unsalted butter, melted

1 egg

Zest of 1 orange

For the Syrup:

1 cup water

1 cup granulated sugar

1 tablespoon lemon juice

1 tablespoon rose water or orange blossom water

NUTRITIONAL INFORMATION
(per serving):

Calories: 320 • **Total Fat:** 10g • **Saturated Fat:** 6g • **Cholesterol:** 45mg • **Sodium:** 65mg • **Total Carbohydrates:** 54g • **Dietary Fiber:** 2g • **Sugars:** 36g • **Protein:** 4g

DIRECTIONS:

1. **Prepare the Cake Batter:**

   a. In a large mixing bowl, combine the semolina, desiccated coconut, sugar, and baking powder. Mix well.

   b. Add the yogurt, melted butter, egg, and orange zest to the dry ingredients. Stir until well combined and a batter is formed.

2. Preheat the air fryer to 350°F (180°C).

3. **Bake the Cake:**

   a. Pour the cake batter into a greased 7-inch round cake pan that fits in your air fryer. Smooth the top with a spatula.

   b. Place the pan in the air fryer basket and cook for 20 minutes or until a toothpick inserted into the center comes out clean.

4. **Prepare the Syrup:** While the cake is cooking, prepare the syrup. In a small saucepan over medium heat, combine the water, sugar, and lemon juice. Bring to a boil, then reduce the heat and simmer for 10 minutes, stirring occasionally, until the syrup thickens slightly. Remove from the heat and stir in the rose water or orange blossom water.

5. **Finish the Cake:** Once the cake is done, remove it from the air fryer and let it cool for 5 minutes. Then, evenly pour the warm syrup over the warm cake, allowing it to soak in.

6. **Serve:** Let the cake cool completely before slicing. Serve garnished with additional desiccated coconut or sliced almonds if desired.

Pomegranate and Pistachio Air-Fried Baklava Rolls

Yield: *12 rolls* | Prep Time: *30 minutes* | Cook Time: *15 minutes*

INGREDIENTS:

1 package phyllo dough, thawed
1 cup pistachios, finely chopped
1/2 cup pomegranate seeds
1/4 cup sugar
1 teaspoon ground cinnamon
1/2 cup unsalted butter, melted

For the Syrup:
1/2 cup water
1 cup sugar
1/2 cup honey
2 tablespoons pomegranate juice
1 teaspoon lemon juice
1 strip lemon zest

NUTRITIONAL INFORMATION
(per roll, approximate):

Calories: 280 • Total Fat: 15g •
Saturated Fat: 6g • Cholesterol:
20mg • Sodium: 120mg • Total
Carbohydrates: 35g • Dietary
Fiber: 2g • Sugars: 25g •
Protein: 4g

DIRECTIONS:

1. **Prepare the Filling:** In a bowl, mix together the finely chopped pistachios, pomegranate seeds, sugar, and ground cinnamon. Set aside.

2. **Prepare the Phyllo Dough:** Lay one sheet of phyllo dough on a clean, flat surface and brush lightly with melted butter. Place another sheet on top and brush again with butter. Repeat this process until you have 4 layers.

3. **Assemble the Rolls:** Spread a portion of the filling along the shorter edge of the layered phyllo sheets. Roll the dough tightly over the filling, forming a log. Slice the log into 3 equal parts to create individual rolls. Repeat with the remaining phyllo sheets and filling.

4. Preheat the air fryer to 350°F (180°C).

5. **Air Fry the Baklava Rolls:**

   a. Lightly spray the air fryer basket with non-stick cooking spray or line it with parchment paper. Place the baklava rolls in the basket, seam side down, ensuring they do not touch. Brush the tops with the remaining melted butter.

   b. Air fry for 12-15 minutes or until the rolls are golden brown and crispy.

6. **Prepare the Syrup:** While the rolls are air frying, combine water, sugar, honey, pomegranate juice, lemon juice, and lemon zest in a saucepan over medium heat. Bring to a boil, then reduce heat and simmer for 10 minutes or until slightly thickened. Remove the lemon zest.

7. **Finish the Baklava Rolls:** Once the baklava rolls are done, immediately drizzle them with the warm pomegranate syrup. Allow the rolls to soak up the syrup for a few minutes before serving.

8. Serve the baklava rolls warm or at room temperature, garnished with additional pomegranate seeds if desired.

Crispy Air-Fried Phyllo Cups with Honey and Nuts

Yield: *12 cups* | Prep Time: *20 minutes* | Cook Time: *5 minutes*

INGREDIENTS:

6 sheets of phyllo dough, thawed
1/4 cup unsalted butter, melted
1/2 cup mixed nuts (walnuts, pistachios, almonds), finely chopped
1/4 cup honey, plus more for drizzling
1/2 teaspoon ground cinnamon
1/4 teaspoon ground cardamom
Powdered sugar for dusting (optional)

DIRECTIONS:

1. **Prepare the Phyllo Sheets:** Carefully lay out one sheet of phyllo dough on a clean, dry surface. Brush lightly with melted butter. Place another sheet on top, brush with butter, and repeat the process until you have 6 layers.

2. **Cut and Shape the Phyllo Cups:** Cut the layered phyllo sheets into 12 squares. Gently press each square into the cups of a mini muffin tin to form a cup shape. If you don't have a mini muffin tin, you can form cups around the outside of an inverted muffin tin.

3. Preheat the air fryer to 350°F (180°C).

4. **Prepare the Filling:** In a bowl, mix the chopped nuts, 1/4 cup honey, cinnamon, and cardamom until well combined.

5. **Fill the Phyllo Cups:** Spoon the nut mixture into the phyllo cups, dividing it evenly among them.

6. **Air Fry the Phyllo Cups:**

   a. Carefully place the filled phyllo cups in the air fryer basket, working in batches if necessary to avoid overcrowding.

   b. Air fry for 4-5 minutes, or until the phyllo is golden and crispy. Watch closely to avoid burning.

7. **Serve:** Let the phyllo cups cool slightly, then carefully remove them from the muffin tin. Drizzle with additional honey and dust with powdered sugar if desired. Serve warm or at room temperature as a delightful dessert or snack.

NUTRITIONAL INFORMATION (per cup):

Calories: 100 • Total Fat: 5g • Saturated Fat: 2g • Cholesterol: 10mg • Sodium: 50mg • Total Carbohydrates: 12g • Dietary Fiber: 1g • Sugars: 6g • Protein: 2g

Air-Fried Mascarpone and Fig Tartlets

Yield: *6 tartlets* | Prep Time: *20 minutes* | Cook Time: *8 minutes*

INGREDIENTS:

For the Tartlet Shells:

1 package (about 14 oz) of pre-made pie dough or puff pastry, thawed

Olive oil spray (for greasing)

For the Filling:

1 cup mascarpone cheese, softened

2 tablespoons honey, plus more for drizzling

1 teaspoon vanilla extract

Zest of 1 lemon

6 fresh figs, quartered

For Garnish:

Chopped pistachios (optional)

Fresh mint leaves (optional)

NUTRITIONAL INFORMATION (per tartlet, approximate):

Calories: 350 • Total Fat: 22g • Saturated Fat: 12g • Cholesterol: 45mg • Sodium: 200mg • Total Carbohydrates: 34g • Dietary Fiber: 2g • Sugars: 16g • Protein: 5g

DIRECTIONS:

1. **Prepare Tartlet Shells:**

   a. Roll out the pie dough or puff pastry on a lightly floured surface. Using a round cutter or a large glass, cut out 6 circles large enough to fit into your tartlet pans or molds.

   b. Press the dough circles into greased tartlet pans or molds, making sure the dough comes up the sides. Prick the bottom of the dough with a fork.

2. Preheat the air fryer to 375°F (190°C).

3. **Air Fry Tartlet Shells:**

   a. Place the tartlet pans in the air fryer basket. You may need to cook them in batches, depending on the size of your air fryer.

   b. Air fry for 6-8 minutes or until the shells are golden and crispy. Let them cool before gently removing them from the pans.

4. **Mix the Filling:** In a bowl, mix together mascarpone cheese, honey, vanilla extract, and lemon zest until smooth.

5. **Assemble the Tartlets:** Spoon the mascarpone filling into the cooled tartlet shells. Arrange the quartered figs on top of the filling.

6. **Serve:** Drizzle with additional honey and sprinkle with chopped pistachios and fresh mint leaves if desired. Serve immediately or chill in the refrigerator until ready to serve.

Mediterranean Olive Oil and Orange Cake

Yield: *6 servings* | Prep Time: *15 minutes* | Cook Time: *20 minutes*

INGREDIENTS:

1 cup all-purpose flour
2/3 cup granulated sugar
1/2 teaspoon baking powder
1/4 teaspoon baking soda
1/4 teaspoon salt
2 large eggs
1/3 cup extra virgin olive oil
Zest of 1 orange
1/4 cup fresh orange juice
1 teaspoon vanilla extract
Powdered sugar for dusting (optional)

NUTRITIONAL INFORMATION
(per serving):

Calories: 280 • Total Fat: 14g •
Saturated Fat: 2g • Cholesterol:
62mg • Sodium: 150mg • Total
Carbohydrates: 36g • Dietary
Fiber: 1g • Sugars: 20g •
Protein: 4g

DIRECTIONS:

1. **Prepare the Batter:**

    a. In a large bowl, whisk together the flour, granulated sugar, baking powder, baking soda, and salt.

    b. In another bowl, beat the eggs lightly. Whisk in the olive oil, orange zest, orange juice, and vanilla extract until well combined.

    c. Pour the wet ingredients into the dry ingredients and stir until just combined, being careful not to overmix.

2. Preheat the air fryer to 320°F (160°C). If your air fryer requires preheating, refer to the manufacturer's instructions.

3. **Prepare the Cake Pan:** Grease a 7-inch round cake pan that fits in your air fryer basket. Line the bottom with parchment paper for easy removal.

4. **Bake the Cake:**

    a. Pour the batter into the prepared pan and smooth the top with a spatula.

    b. Place the pan in the air fryer basket and cook for 18-20 minutes, or until a toothpick inserted into the center of the cake comes out clean. The cooking time may vary depending on the air fryer model.

5. **Cool and Serve:** Allow the cake to cool in the pan for about 10 minutes before transferring it to a wire rack to cool completely. Dust with powdered sugar before serving, if desired.

Chapter 10

How to create

a Mediterranean Diet Meal Plan
for Optimal Health

Embark on a Journey to Wellness

Crafting Your Mediterranean Diet Meal Plan

Creating a personalized Mediterranean diet meal plan is not just about selecting the right foods; it's about embracing a lifestyle that values mealtime as an opportunity for enjoyment and socialization. This guide will provide you with a step-by-step approach to designing a meal plan that not only adheres to the principles of the Mediterranean diet but also fits into your individual lifestyle, preferences, and nutritional needs. Whether you're looking to improve your heart health, lose weight, or simply adopt a more balanced diet, this guide is your starting point towards a healthier, more vibrant life.

1. Understand the Essentials of the Mediterranean Diet

Begin your voyage by immersing yourself in the core principles of the Mediterranean diet. This heart-healthy diet emphasizes:

BOUNTIFUL FRUITS AND VEGETABLES
Feast on a colorful array of produce, making them the cornerstone of your meals.

WHOLE GRAINS GALORE
Incorporate grains like farro, barley, and whole-grain pasta into your diet.

THE RICHNESS OF HEALTHY FATS
Revel in the goodness of olive oil, nuts, and seeds.

LEAN PROTEINS
Enjoy portions of seafood, poultry, and plant-based proteins such as legumes.

DAIRY DELIGHTS
Opt for fermented dairy products like Greek yogurt and small amounts of cheese.

FLAVORFUL HERBS AND SPICES
Season your dishes with herbs like oregano, basil, and mint for a burst of flavor without the salt.

2. Set your daily caloric needs:

2.1 CALCULATE BASAL METABOLIC RATE (BMR):

BMR is an estimated number of calories your body needs daily while at rest. Several equations can be used to calculate BMR, with the Harris-Benedict equation being one of the most commonly used. Here's a simplified version:

For Men: $BMR = 88.362 + (13.397 \times weight\ in\ kg) + (4.799 \times height\ in\ cm) - (5.677 \times age\ in\ years)$

For Women: $BMR = 447.593 + (9.247 \times weight\ in\ kg) + (3.098 \times height\ in\ cm) - (4.330 \times age\ in\ years)$

2.2 ADJUST FOR ACTIVITY LEVEL:

To establish the total daily need for calories is necessary to consider your physical activity level. Multiply your BMR by the factor that best represents your activity level:

Sedentary (little or no exercise):
BMR x 1.2

Lightly active (light exercise/sports 1-3 days a week):
BMR x 1.375

Moderately active (moderate exercise/sports 3-5 days a week):
BMR x 1.55

Very active (hard exercise/sports 6-7 days a week):
BMR x 1.725

Extra active (very hard exercise/sports and a physical job):
BMR x 1.9

The result you get is your final daily calorie requirement.

3. Based on your caloric needs, distribute your intake across the Mediterranean diet's food groups:

Grains: 6-8 servings/day

Vegetables: 4-5 servings/day

Fruits: 4-5 servings/day

Dairy: 2-3 servings/day (low-fat or non-fat)

Proteins: Fish, poultry, and legumes, aiming for variety and moderation

Nuts/Seeds: A handful several times a week

Oils: Mainly olive oil, 2-3 servings/day

4. Adjust Based on Goals:

If your goal is to lose weight, you'll want to create a caloric deficit by consuming fewer calories, increasing physical activity, or both. Conversely, you'll need a caloric surplus if you're going to gain weight or muscle.

Track your food intake and physical activity, and adjust as needed based on your progress and goals.

For personalized recommendations and monitoring, consult with a registered dietitian or nutritionist.

5. Mapping Out Your Mediterranean Meals

Strategize your weekly meal plan with these guidelines to ensure a diverse and delicious menu:

MORNING MERRIMENT
Kick-start your day with fiber-rich grains, fruits, and proteins.

LUSCIOUS LUNCHES AND DINNERS
Anchor your main meals with vegetables, complemented by whole grains and lean proteins. Drizzle with olive oil for a heart-healthy fat boost.

SNACK SMARTLY
Choose snacks that provide energy and nutrients, such as a handful of almonds or a piece of fruit.

6. Sample Meal Plan

MONDAY

Breakfast: Whole grain toast with avocado and poached eggs.

Lunch: Grilled vegetable and quinoa salad with olive oil and lemon dressing.

Dinner: Baked salmon with roasted Brussels sprouts and sweet potatoes.

TUESDAY

Breakfast: Greek yogurt with honey, nuts, and berries.

Lunch: Chickpea and spinach stew with whole grain bread.

Dinner: Grilled chicken with a side of mixed greens salad and farro.

Repeat the process for the rest of the week, ensuring variety.

7. Grocery Shopping

- Make a list based on your meal plan.

- Prioritize fresh and seasonal produce, whole grains, and lean proteins.

- Stock up on staples like olive oil, nuts, seeds, and legumes.

8. Masterful Meal Preparation: Enhancing Your Mediterranean Diet Experience

A well-organized meal preparation strategy not only saves time throughout the week but also ensures that you adhere to your Mediterranean diet meal plan with ease and enjoyment. Here's how you can master your cooking routine:

8.1 BATCH COOKING: THE FOUNDATION OF EFFORTLESS MEALS

Grains and Legumes: Select a day to cook grains such as quinoa, brown rice, farro, and legumes like lentils and chickpeas. These can serve as the base for a variety of dishes, from salads to stir-fries, which you will cook throughout the week. Cook them in bulk and store them in portioned containers in the fridge or freezer.

- *How to cook Grains: Rinse your grains thoroughly. Use from 2:1 to 3:1 ratio of water to grains, depending on the grain type, bring to a boil, then simmer until tender. This usually takes about 15-30 minutes.*

- **How to cook Legumes**: *Soak dried beans overnight to reduce cooking time. Rinse, then cook in fresh water until tender, which can vary from 1 to 2 hours depending on the legume type. Alternatively, use canned beans for convenience, ensuring they're rinsed well to reduce sodium content.*

8.2 VEGETABLE PREPARATION: ENSURING FRESHNESS AND ACCESSIBILITY

Wash and Chop: Clean your vegetables as soon as you bring them home from the market. Chop, dice, or slice them based on how you plan to use them during the week. Store them in clear containers in the fridge to keep them visible and easily accessible.

HOW TO PREP VEGETABLES EFFICIENTLY:

- **Leafy Greens**: *Wash in a large bowl of cold water, dry thoroughly (a salad spinner works great), and store wrapped in a paper towel inside a resealable bag.*

- **Root Vegetables**: *Peel if necessary, then chop or dice. Root vegetables like carrots and beets can also be roasted in advance and added to meals as needed.*

- **Herbs**: *Wrap in a damp paper towel and store in a resealable bag. They can also be chopped and frozen in olive oil in ice cube trays.*

8.3 PORTION CONTROL: BALANCING YOUR MEALS

Mindful Portions: Understanding portion sizes is crucial, especially for higher-calorie foods like nuts, seeds, and olive oil. Use measure spoons and cups or a kitchen scale to help manage portions.

PORTION CONTROL TIPS:

- **Healthy Fats**: *For olive oil, a serving size is typically 1 tablespoon. Use a spray bottle for cooking or dressing salads to control the amount used.*

- **Nuts and Seeds**: *A serving size is usually about 1 ounce or a small handful. Pre-portion these into snack bags or containers for easy access and to prevent overeating.*

- **Cheese**: *Opt for small portions about the size of a dice, especially if you're including cheese in meals or as a snack.*

By integrating these meal preparation strategies into your weekly routine, you can simplify your Mediterranean diet meal plan, making it easier to enjoy nutritious, homemade meals every day. This approach not only helps in maintaining a healthy diet but also reduces stress and decision fatigue about meal choices throughout the week.

9. Stay Hydrated

Drink plenty of water throughout the day. Stay well-hydrated with water, herbal teas, and other low-sugar beverages. Enjoy moderate amounts of red wine, if desired and appropriate for your health. While the Mediterranean diet does not strictly limit caffeine, moderate its intake if you're sensitive to its effects.

10. Mindful Eating

Take the time to savor your meals. Slow down and appreciate the flavors of your food. Listen to your body's hunger and fullness cues.

11. Integration of Physical Activity

Pair your Mediterranean diet plan with regular physical activity for comprehensive health benefits. Consult with healthcare professionals to tailor dietary and exercise plans to your individual needs, ensuring a holistic approach to improving your health.

12. Regularly Review and Adjust Your Plan

Keep track of your eating habits, physical activity, how you feel, and any changes in your health metrics. Adjust your meal plan as needed to ensure it continues to meet your health and wellness goals.

ADDITIONAL TIPS:

Enjoy meals with family or friends when possible, as communal eating is a key aspect of the Mediterranean lifestyle.

Adopting the Mediterranean diet is more than just eating certain foods; it's about embracing a lifestyle that prioritizes health, enjoyment of food, and shared meals.

This guide offers a structured approach to adopting the Mediterranean diet, emphasizing its key components, meal planning, preparation tips, and the importance of enjoying the process and the meals.

By following these steps, you can create a Mediterranean diet meal plan that not only improves your health but also brings enjoyment and variety to your daily eating habits.

Welcome to your Mediterranean journey toward a healthier, happier life.

Chapter 11

Measurement Conversion Chart

U.S. SYSTEM	METRIC
1 inch	2.54 centimeters
1 fluid ounce	29.57 milliliters
1 pint (16 ounces, 1cups)	473.18 milliliters
1 quart (32 ounces, 4 cups)	1 liter
1 gallon (128 ounces, 16 cups)	4 liter
1 pound (16 ounces)	453.6 grams (0.4536 kilograms),
1 ounce (2 tablespoons)	28.35 grams
1 cup (8 ounces)	237 milliliters
1 teaspoon	5 milliliters
1 tablespoon (3 teaspoons)	15 milliliters
Fahrenheit to Centigrade: subtract 32 and divide by 1.8 to get Celsius.	Centigrade to Fahrenheit: multiply by 1.8 and add 32 to get Fahrenheit

Conclusion

As we close the pages of this culinary journey through the Mediterranean Air Fryer Diet Cookbook, it's my hope that you've discovered not just a collection of recipes but a new perspective on cooking and eating that enriches your life.

The fusion of Mediterranean traditions with the modern convenience of air frying offers a pathway to meals that are both nourishing and delightful, proving that a commitment to health does not mean sacrificing flavor or pleasure at the dining table.

The recipes within these pages were crafted with love and care, aiming to bring the vibrant colors, rich flavors, and nutritional wealth of the Mediterranean diet into your daily routine, all while leveraging the efficiency and health benefits of air frying. From crispy falafel to tender fish, savory vegetables, and sweet treats, each dish has been a testament to the fact that eating well can be a joyous affair.

As you continue to explore the possibilities of your air fryer and the bounty of Mediterranean cuisine, remember that cooking is an adventure — one that is as much about the journey as it is about the destination. Let curiosity guide you, let flavors inspire you, and let health and happiness be your companions along the way.

Thank you for allowing me, Ellen Ruell, to be a part of your culinary exploration. May your kitchen be a place of discovery, your table a place of connection, and your meals a source of joy and vitality. Here's to many more delicious adventures ahead, embracing the best of the Mediterranean with the ease and innovation of air frying. Buon appetito and happy cooking!

We have a small favor to ask before you embark on your culinary journey. Please take a few minutes to leave your opinion on our book on Amazon. Your feedback is very precious to us and helps us improve. Thank you and all the best!

Made in United States
Troutdale, OR
01/25/2025